BUT, GOD...

I'M NOT AN INTERCESSOR!!

A Fervent Cry To The
Church To Realign Itself
To Fulfill Its Destiny!

Denise M. Carey

PRESS

But, God... I'm Not An Intercessor!!
A Fervent Cry To The Church To Realign Itself To Fulfill Its Destiny!
by Denise M. Carey

Printed in the United States of America

ISBN 978-1-60647-420-4

Unless otherwise indicated, Bible quotations are taken from The Nelson Study Bible, New King James Version. Copyright © 1997 by Thomas Nelson Inc.

www.xulonpress.com

Dedication

To the two most important people in my life. My son, Michael, who God taught patience and perseverance, at a very early age, and Mark, my best friend and confidante who God has transformed into an awesome man of faith. I am so thankful and blessed to have you in my life.

TABLE OF CONTENTS   PAGE NUMBER

Acknowledgements

Shortly after I came to know the Lord as my Savior, I was told that I was an intercessor. This revelation was given to me by a few individuals who were shepherding me in my "early years." I was then given a prophetic word of confirmation by a prophet, Dennis Cramer, that I was indeed an intercessor. I will go into a more detail in the introduction regarding the prophecy. At that time, I began to realize God took this intercessory gift very seriously. I thought it would be wise to follow His lead and do the same.

Over the past decade, I have diligently sought to understand intercession and what this gift means to the Church today. I have been tremendously blessed by the godly people God has placed in my life, as well as the incredible resources available on the vital subject of intercession.

I have a high regard and the deepest appreciation for leaders and authors such as Bill Johnson, John Paul Jackson, Cindy Jacobs, Dutch Sheets, Chuck Pierce, James Goll, Jill Austin, Eddie and Alice Smith, Paul Keith Davis, Rick Joyner, and the list goes on. I praise God for these mighty warriors. Many of you have been pastors from afar to me. Thank you.

My desire is not to duplicate what these generals in God's army have written, but, rather to speak to two specific areas that have significantly impacted my walk with God.

First, I strongly believe that an overwhelming number of gifted and anointed intercessors are sitting in (or perhaps outside!) the church today who have no idea they are mighty intercessors. I pray that this book reaches these people and that God anoints every word I write to bring them much needed revelation and release.

Second, I want to address the issue of "awakened intercessors" who are out there, but are not walking in the fullness of their calling. They are not walking in their God-given authority due to misunderstandings, confusion or feelings of inadequacy.

In all of this, I see a broken link that needs to be mended between the gift of intercession and the gift of prophecy. Many leaders have reported that the gift of prophecy has not been fully restored in the body of Christ. I agree; I believe that a part of this problem is because the gift of *intercession* has not been fully restored. The enemy has been in the Church, deceiving God's people regarding this incredible gift of intercession. I pray that this book will touch these precious people and bring understanding, clarity and wisdom. In Jesus' name.

Because of the Cross.

"And being in agony, He (Jesus) prayed more earnestly. Then His sweat became like great drops of blood falling down to the ground" (Luke 22:44 NKJ).

"PRAY FOR ONE ANOTHER" (James 5:16 NKJ).

Introduction:

On October 23, 2001, I received a personal prophecy from a man after God's heart, by the name of Dennis Cramer, who came to Saskatoon, Saskatchewan to deliver God's words of life and freedom to some very thirsty people. I was one of those thirsty people!

I won't share the entire prophecy, just the portions that were the seeds for this book.

> "...I've got a bunch of neat things to tell you, and I'll start right from the top.. Intercessor, intercessor, intercessor, intercessor, intercessor, ...intercessor, intercessor. ...Have I not made you a gifted woman? Have I not given you creative skills? Have I not put a book in your belly? You'll write that book. And it will be a book, says the Lord, that sets captives free!"

I must admit, at this time the prophecy was given over me, I didn't think there was a book inside me waiting to be written. I thought the person sitting beside me would probably write a book and Dennis Cramer simply missed it by one person. After all, though Dennis Cramer was apparently very accurate with his first several prophecies he couldn't be right all the time, could he? The strange thing was, this prophetic word wouldn't go away.

Over the years, these words grew inside me. What I didn't know is that this prophetic word penetrated my spirit, and a seed was planted. My mind rejected it, but my spirit took it in.

Fast-forward to August, 2007. I was surfing the Internet and came across some computer software for writing books. At the very same time, my dear friend, Mark, purchased a state-of-the-art notebook for me. I know—he's terrific! He said he felt an urgency for the "book" to be written. By then I did, too. The problem was, I wasn't sure what God wanted me to write. I was waiting for this life-changing visitation from the Lord when He would supernaturally download the book in its entirety. I thought it would be great if He gave it to me page by page, word for word, but that was not the case. Ultimately, the writing is part of the journey, the faith walk, the adventure. After all, our walk is one of faith and courage. And a walk of total dependency on Him. Amen.

My prayer is that those who read this book would be blessed. I don't want to do anything out of my own strength and understanding. I want this to be an anointed venture and pray that this book brings freedom to the captives—to the Church. Yes, the Church is in desperate need of freedom and release. I am trusting God will use this vessel to that end. I know it is not up to me, but it is all about God. My part is to take a step of faith and of obedience. Be blessed and be set free!

Part One

Intercession

Chapter 1

Demystifying Intercession

Shortly after I was saved, the gift of intercession was flowing through me, but I had little understanding at that time, as to what was happening. I could sense and see things others could not. I could "read" people, sometimes with incredible precision, and many of my prayers were answered quickly. I knew that all of what was happening was God, but beyond that I wasn't sure what to do with it. Looking back, that had both positive and negative consequences. On the positive side, the Holy Spirit had freedom to move through me, a vessel, who had no pre-conceived notions of how the anointing should look. I could disengage from the process on an intellectual basis and allow the Holy Spirit to do what He wanted. On the down side, however, I lacked wisdom and discernment and therefore opened the door for Satan to attack and for man to judge (not fun).

Over the years, I have had both (spiritual and emotional) bumps and bruises along this journey of intercession. And while I am sure there will be more along the way, I see it as a good thing, because it keeps me dependent upon Him.

I want to share some of my experiences thus far, both the good and the not so good, in hopes of demystifying the gift of intercession. Further, for those who are starting out on this path, I want to point out and help them avoid some of the pitfalls along the way, hoping they will have an easier transition into the incredible gift of intercession.

I would like to start by identifying some lies that were spoken to me regarding intercession:

Lie #1—

"Only seasoned, spiritually mature Christians are anointed with the gift of intercession."

In my early years, I met a pastor who said that "I was too young in the Lord" to be an intercessor. At the time I certainly lacked wisdom as all baby Christians do, and my character needed refinement (okay, perhaps an overhaul would be a more accurate description), but I had already been gifted as an intercessor nonetheless. I just needed loving correction and discipline to bring me to maturity. But because I allowed them to have power over me this man's words brought condemnation and quenched what God was doing until someone finally spoke the truth. And the truth is it is up to God whom He anoints with what gift and for what purpose.

"There are diversities of gifts, but the same Spirit. There are differences of ministries, but the same Lord" (1 Corinthians 12: 4-5 NKJ).

God doesn't restrict the anointing to only those who are spiritually mature. He doesn't limit gifts only to those who have gone to Bible school, spent ten or more years studying the Word, and whom elders and leaders deem worthy. It's a good thing He doesn't. I have to wonder who would actually be anointed for the work of God if this were so. I know I wouldn't.

Here are some examples of those who God chooses:

God's chosen people were the Jews. In man's eyes, they appeared to be a pathetic and forsaken nation. God also chose Paul, a former Pharisee and persecutor of Christians—another example that seems strange. In truth, Christ's disciples weren't all well-educated ministers; they were laborers, blue-collar workers. Matthew was a tax collector. Peter was a fisherman.

His ways are not our ways. He knows the beginning from the end, while we see only a small part of His plan. I am so thankful for His ways, His love, His mercy, His grace!

"Bear one another's burdens, and so fulfill the law of Christ" (Galatians 6:2 NKJ).

In fact, bearing one another's burdens is precisely what God expects from every believer. I recognize now that intercessory prayer is what matured me and created a hunger to press into God and His Word. While I interceded for someone, God would often reveal His heart for me and through the process, heal me. The more I prayed for others, the more that revelation became clear.

Lie # 2—

"Groaning and travailing will offend unbelievers and some Christians, so don't do it."

Another experience I had involved a fellow believer. A few of us had begun to gather together to wait upon the Lord. Our prayer times had become a regular practice, and our numbers were growing. When we met the Spirit of the

Lord would come down, bringing manifestations of the Spirit, including groaning and travailing, which then brought healing of past hurts, and some were even filled with the Holy Spirit!

At that point someone approached me prior to a session and said there would be more conservative Christians present, and the groaning would be offensive to them. Clearly this individual was hoping that it wouldn't happen. Again, because I was vulnerable I allowed these words to have power and as a result, condemnation and fear flooded my spirit and in an instant shut things down. Needless to say, the Holy Spirit wasn't flowing through me that night, groaning, travailing or in any other way. Through these experiences I learned that I had allowed negative words to impact my relationship with the Holy Spirit at least temporarily. It wasn't the words alone, though, it was my response to the words that gave them power—ultimately giving Satan power instead of God.

I also discovered there is a difference between a wound in my soul and a wound in my spirit. I can usually get over a "soul" wound fairly quickly. I choose to forgive the individual who has wounded me then ask God to reveal the area in my soul that needs healing and its "root cause." I will pray for that person, asking God to bless him. Spiritual wounds, however, go much, much deeper. Spiritual wounds attack the anointing, the Spirit of the Lord within me. Many of the lies regarding intercession that were spoken to me wounded me on a spiritual level. And the only way I could be healed from them was to spend time "soaking" in His presence and receiving a revelatory word to address the situation. Many times, I wouldn't even be aware of the wound until I soaked and God exposed the wound. Satan's attacks are often insidious; deception is his favorite method of attack.

In reality, there will be situations and manifestations that will offend some people. At that point one of two things can happen. The offense will expose something in their heart that needs to be broken, and if they submit to God, they will be set free.

"Now the Lord is the Spirit, and where the Spirit of the Lord is, there is liberty" (II Corinthians 3: 17 NKJ)

If freedom doesn't come, the offense may anger them and expose the enemy in their lives. This, most likely, will be a religious spirit or another demonic spirit creating the offense.

The gospel itself often brings offense. The cross brings offense because it speaks of God's unmerited grace, which leaves absolutely no room for our good works.

"And I, brethren, if I still preach circumstances, why do I still suffer persecution? Then the offense of the cross has ceased" (Galatians 5:11 NKJ).

Intercession, along with all other aspects of the character of Jesus, will bring offense. I guarantee it. When opposing kingdoms collide, there will be a resulting clash!

Lie# 3—

"The person who is interceding will know who, or what, they are interceding for. Otherwise it's not God."

Another lie from the enemy. At times, someone would ask what I was weeping about, or in travail for. If I couldn't give any insight into what was going on, I was told that it wasn't the Lord, and that it must be the enemy.

Over the years I found that sometimes God gives me revelation and very specific knowledge regarding the purpose of the intercession, while other times He is silent and reveals nothing. I may have a general sense of something, such as a feeling of urgency to pray in tongues, or perhaps a feeling of sorrow. When I can't attribute the emotion to anything going on in my life, I will spend time with the Lord in prayer inquiring regarding what direction He wants me to take. What I have discovered is that He wants to create dependency upon Him so I stay close to Him—under His wing. After spending time with Him, He may reveal something, while at other times I may get no further insight. I have come to understand that sometimes it's none of my business to know what I'm praying! God is in control, and that's all that matters.

"For My thoughts are not your thoughts, nor are your ways My ways, says the Lord. For as the heavens are higher than the earth, so are My ways higher than your ways, and My thoughts than your thoughts" (Isaiah 55: 8-9 NKJ).

"For we do not know what we should pray for as we ought, but the Spirit Himself makes intercession for us with groanings which cannot be uttered" (Romans 8:26 NKJ).

Lie # 4—

"The intercession can be turned on and off by the intercessor."

There is an element of truth to this statement. We can say yes to the Lord and receive the mantel of intercession. We can also decline an occasion where God will ask us to intercede on behalf of someone. We can also shut down the flow of intercession as mentioned earlier, by quenching the Holy Spirit and allowing Satan to have control. In certain instances it is necessary to control the manifestations of the spirit. When in a church or corporate setting where the joy of the Lord is flowing, this is not the time or place to quench what the Holy Spirit is doing in others. God will give you the grace and strength to contain the intercessory burden so that there is freedom for the flow of His Spirit in all directions. Many times, I feel like a fish out of water in corporate settings. I want to weep when others are laughing; I want to wage war when others are celebrating. But I have grace from God, not to quench what the Holy Spirit is doing. I can still intercede without impeding the corporate flow. This is especially true of prophetic intercessors; you will continually feel out of step with others, because God has you praying for something that has yet to come.

Another time I was praying in a small home group. Because the leaders were speaking on the gifts of the Holy Spirit and different manifestations of the Holy Spirit they thought it would be helpful to demonstrate what this would look like. The group included those who were new believers and had never had any personal experiences with such things, while others had had personal experiences with evil spirits. When the leaders began to pray that the Lord would release a gift of intercession, my heart went out to a woman who was in bondage, with a history of victimization and abuse. In response to that request the Lord had by now begun to reveal some specific bondages that He wanted to break in this woman, when suddenly the leaders stopped the process as if it were merely a demonstration of tears and travail rather than the real thing. They weren't expecting God to use this time to actually heal and deliver!

And though God had shown up in power, He honored the leadership, and as quickly as it had come the anointing lifted.

This was definitely a learning experience for all us. Thankfully, the pastor brought us together after the incident, and the discussion resulted in reconciliation and healing so the enemy couldn't use the situation to bring condemnation or injury.

I have also learned that once the travail in the spirit has been released, it is not easy to shut it off. In the spirit, something is being birthed. Just as in the natural, once labor has begun, the woman cannot simply decide to stop things at her whim. God is in control!

"I am weary with my groaning; all night I make my bed swim; I drench my couch with my tears" (Psalm 6:6 NKJ).

Lie # 5 —

"Some forms of intercession are acceptable and others are not."

I have found that some churches and individuals are alright with the holy laughter and other manifestations that are considered positive or enjoyable. But the forms of intercession such as weeping, groaning, travail or expressions that may be viewed as a little "out there" or sorrowful are not accepted and ultimately, are judged by those who don't understand them. Because we are human we all have a tendency to judge and discredit what we don't understand or what is out of our comfort zone. But this is where we need wisdom from God.

"The fear of the Lord is the beginning or wisdom, and the knowledge of the Holy One is understanding" (Proverbs 9:10 NKJ).

"These things also belong to the wise: It is not good to show partiality in judgment" (Proverbs 24: 23).

I think of the scripture in Ecclesiastes 3 (My friend Mark calls this the Book of Elastics!), where it says there is a time and season for everything. There is a time to laugh and a time to mourn. Both emotions are used by the Lord to break down strongholds. To shut off one emotion is to shut off an essential aspect of God's character. Granted, we as believers do not mourn the same way unbelievers do, but then we don't dance in the same way as unbelievers do either!

Lie # 6—

"Men cannot be intercessors."

I'm really not sure why some people believe this lie. Perhaps it is an attempt to get off the hook rather than spend time in prayer. Unfortunately, most prayer and intercessory groups are predominantly made up of women. But I have male friends that are definitely intercessors; some are even "birthers"! The Bible tells us about many male intercessors: Moses, Ezekiel, Samuel, Joseph, Elijah, Elisha, and the list goes on and on.

My friend, Mark, is an intercessor, but he isn't a "birther," so the intercession doesn't manifest through groaning or travail. He is a warrior. When he intercedes, he declares the Word of God into the heavenlies, and there are dramatic breakthroughs. My son is an intercessor with a quiet demeanor whose intercession simply leaks out without much outward evidence. I have learned that intercession is not a one-size fits-all proposition, but that it merely looks different on different people.

I have also seen spiritual gifts inherited within families. Chances are that if your mother or father or grandparents were intercessors, you are, too.

Lie # 7 —

"Only 10% of the Church is intercessors."

I have heard over the years that approximately 8-10% of the Church is gifted in intercession. Where do these lies come from? Right—from Satan who is the father of lies! An easy way of thwarting prayer and breakthroughs for the Body of Christ is to stop people from interceding for others.

Lie # 8 -

"The gift of intercession is really not that important or is somehow unworthy."

I'm not sure if I have worded this lie accurately, but I have come across this lie repeatedly. It is usually not expressed verbally, but certain people believe that prayer and intercession are boring, not at all enjoyable. Because of that they believe He has left this gift to little old ladies who life has already passed by, those with nothing but time on their hands. To that I say hogwash! Intercession is incredible and a very intimate experience. An intercessor is privileged to tap into the Father's heart and should feel blessed, overwhelmed with gratitude and downright undone by God's enormous heart. I am so thankful each day for the gift of intercession. I fall in love with God more and more each day I pray.

Lie # 9 -

"The gift of intercession is boring, and it is done out of a sense of duty."

I see this with other commandments that God has given us. For example, tithing is a requirement for Christians. Many Christians don't consider tithing a joy or rewarding, merely a commandment to follow out of obligation. But the truth is, when God commands, and we comply with cheerful, willing hearts we will be amazingly blessed. And there is tremendous joy to be gained in submitting to His authority! I would like to offer a prayer right now.

Lord, if readers have listened to lies regarding what intercession is or how it is suppose to look, I ask that You would expose these lies right now, Holy Spirit. Reveal truth and bring healing in these areas. We forgive those who have spoken these lies and speak blessing and truth to them as well, in Jesus' name. If we ourselves have spoken any of these lies toward others, forgive us. Bring revelation and restoration to your children. Heal them in body, soul and spirit. In Jesus' mighty name. Amen.

Chapter 2

What is Intercession?

William Law (1686-1761) was an English Christian writer. His writings impacted many writers and teachers such as John and Charles Wesley and George MacDonald. In his book *A Serious Call To A Devout And Holy Life* (1728), he wrote:

"That intercession is a great and necessary part of Christian devotion is very evident from Scripture. The first followers of Christ seem to support all their love, and to maintain all their intercourse and correspondence, by mutual prayers for one another. St. Paul, whether he writes to churches or particular persons, shows his intercession to be perpetual for them, that they are the constant subject of his prayers. Thus to the Philippians, 'I thank my God upon every remembrance of you, always in every prayer of mine for you making all requests with joy.' (Phil. 1:3-4).

Here we see not only a continual intercession, but performed with so much gladness, as shows that it was an exercise of love in which he highly rejoiced. His devotion had also the same care for particular persons, as appears by the following passages: 'I thank God, whom I serve from my forefathers, with a pure conscience, that without ceasing I have remembrance of thee in my prayers night and day' (2 Tim. 1:3).

Apostles and great saints did not only thus benefit and bless particular churches and private persons, but they themselves also received graces from God by the prayer of others. Thus says St. Paul to the Corinthians: "You also helping together by prayer for us, that for the gift bestowed upon us by the means of many persons, thanks may be given by many on our behalf' (2 Cor. 1:11). This was the ancient friendship of Christians, uniting and cementing their hearts, not by worldly considerations, or human passions, but by the mutual communication of spiritual blessings, by prayers and thanksgivings to God for one another.

It was holy intercession that raised Christians to such a state of mutual love, as far exceeded all that had been praised and admired in human friendship. And when the same spirit of intercession is again in the world, when Christianity has the same power over the hearts of people that it then had, this holy friendship will again be in fashion, and Christians will be again the wonder of the world, for that exceeding love which they bear to one another. For a frequent intercession with God, earnestly beseeching Him to forgive the sins of all mankind, to bless them with His providence, enlighten them with His Spirit, and bring them to everlasting happiness, is the divinest exercise that the heart of man can be engaged in." (1)

Paul Cain, who has a calling of a prophet, once stated the following:

"There will be no public reaping without some public weeping. The greatest reapers in this world are the greatest weepers.

28

There is a gift that we need to ask God for in these days. It's the gift of tears. We need to come before the Lord, making ourselves available to Him in a deeper way. The gift of tears is more than a result of the suffering that comes from living in a fallen world. It flows from feeling the pain and the suffering that the Lord Jesus feels for us. He is our High Priest, touched by the feeling our infirmities. We need to feel what He feels for America. We need to feel what He feels for the Church. We need to feel what He feels about sin and the abominations that are going on in the earth today.

We must have tears if we are going to see revival. If we have no tears it's because our hearts are parched. Lord give us tears that we may see revival!

David said in Psalm 6, 'I'm worn out from groaning all night long. How long has it been since you or I have groaned all night long? He also said, I flood my bed with weeping and drench my couch with tears. My eyes grow weak with sorrow.

Have you considered Jesus Christ as man of sorrows? He's not known as a man of laughter. He's not known as a man of frivolous flippancy. He is known as a man of sorrows.

Oh, for prophets like Jeremiah, who cried out for his eyes to be a fountain of tears! Prayer and intercession is our most important work. Let that be locked into your thinking.

Prayer and intercession is the most important work of the Church." (2)

Jill Austin, author and prophetess, and founder of Master Potter Ministries, describes the Old Testament judge, Deborah as an intercessor. Jill writes:

"Deborah stood in the gap and interceded to change the course of Israel. God promised Abraham, in Genesis 18, that He would save a nation for the sake of ten righteous men. It's clear that the righteous prayers of Deborah availed much!

She worshipped and had a deep intercessory prayer life with God. She would go into the temple and fill the lamps with oil and ask God for revelation for people around her in great darkness. She was prepared in this secret place as she stood in the gap in radical intercession for her people and her nation. She would hear from God and would bring down great wisdom and counsel. She spent long hours in the temple. This dedication moved the very heart of God and changed the very heart of Deborah. He led, she followed. She led, Israel followed.

Oftentimes we have the misunderstanding that worship is merely the thirty-minute time slot before the sermon when we sing songs of devotion to God. This is part of worship. But when we do small things with great love for Him, this, too, is living a life of worship. Deborah was a worshipper who loved the true oil of the lamps, the Holy Spirit.

We need to be like Deborah, a people of mighty prayer. Sincere and passionate prayer is the key to unlocking our relationship with God. Many struggle with praying because they feel that their intercession is not much more than empty cries to an invisible God who seems so distant. We often believe our prayers bounce off the ceiling and back to us unheard and unanswered. But beloved, God loves communing with you! He promises that He will hear you and answer! It takes only a few seconds of a face-to-face encounter with God to change the course of human history for you, your city, or your nation.

In fact, communing with God, is the highest purpose for which you were created! This is eternal life to know Me. (John 17:3) Our hunger for God is what fuels our prayer life. When His presence is our passion and our hunger is for His heart, we can approach the throne of God boldly with the confidence that our Daddy loves our prayers, but having this first love is so important.

For Deborah, intercession was a dialogue in which He began to download strategic war plans, blue prints from heaven, and keys to open doors that no man can shut and shut doors that no man can open. (Isa. 22:22) How else could she wisely judge so many civil cases with the Israelites?" (3)

Eddie and Alice Smith, the founders of the U.S. Prayer Centre, define intercessors this way: "We stand in the gap between what is (the need) and what should be (God's will). We intercede on behalf of people, crisis situations, and nations. We also intercede for righteousness where we see unrighteousness, for mercy where we see unforgiveness, for love where we see hate, for grace where there is need, and so on. The Holy Spirit knows the gaps that the Father desires for us to fill. So He gives us a burden for that which we should pray." (4)

Andrew Smith, a revivalist from the nineteenth century wrote the following:

"The Holy Spirit has been bestowed by the Father to breathe the very Spirit of His Son into our hearts. Our Lord desires us to yield ourselves as wholly to God as He did- to pray as He did, that God's will of love would be done on earth at any cost. As God's love is revealed in His desire for the salvation of souls, so also the desire of Jesus was made plain when He gave Himself for them. And He now asks that the same love would fill His people, too, so that they give themselves wholly to the work of intercession and, at any cost, pray down God's love upon the perishing world." (5)

Chuck Pierce describes himself as an intercessor. He is the President of Glory of Zion International Ministries and Vice President of Global Harvest Ministries. He describes his ultimate call as intercession. He writes:

"The call of God is progressive. This actually means that you have a starting place, but God matures you into the fullness of His plan. God has a plan over each one of our lives. He also has a plan for people groups and a plan for nations. When He is knitting us together on our mother's womb, that plan is being initiated. The call of God is the highest part of God's plan for us individually. God then matures our individual call as we align corporately in the Body of Christ. We were never meant to be independent. God made us so that our gifts and destinies would align with others. The hand needs the arm; the eyes need the mind; and so on. Once we find our place in the Body of Christ and we see that 'room has been made for our gift,' our call is extended to the city and territory that we are a part of. As we become stewards and faithful to demonstrate God's covenant plan in every aspect of our life, He can extend our call even to a nation. Therefore, the functionality of our gift can increase and be used in a greater scope, function, or sphere of authority. (6)

I believe this is true. And I believe that it all begins with intercession — intercession that connects to the Father's heart.

There are incredible resources out there regarding intercession. As I mentioned in the introduction, my intention is not to duplicate what is already available. I have included a list of resources at the end of this book. But before I go further, I want to cover the basics.

1) Jesus is our Chief Intercessor!

Jesus is our model to follow. Intercessory prayer is His chief ministry. He is the mediator between us and God.

"Who, in the days of His flesh, when He had offered up prayers and supplications, with vehement cries and tears to Him who was able to save Him from death, and was heard because of His godly fear, though He was a Son, yet He learned obedience by the things which He suffered" (Hebrews 5:7-8 NKJ).

"Therefore, He is also able to save to the uttermost those who come to God through Him, since He always lives to make intercession for them" (Hebrews 7:25 NKJ).

2) God Seeks out Intercessors!

God rules the world and His church through intercession. He extends His kingdom through the intercessory prayer of His people. God seeks out intercessors. In fact He has made His work dependent upon the fervent cries of those who pray.

"And He saw that there was no man; and wondered that there was no intercessor" (Isaiah 59:16 NKJ).

3) Our World is Shaped by Intercessory Prayer!

Simply put, if there is something in your life or in the life of a loved one that is contrary to the will of God, pray the will of God into that situation. If your neighborhood has a high rate of crime, intercessory prayer can change your community.

At one time, there was an adult video store in my neighborhood. Every chance I had I spoke over that building that God's kingdom would be released. The store is now closed! That is one small example of what prayer can accomplish. You came into the Kingdom through intercessory prayer. Nothing is too small or too big for our God. He makes the impossible possible, and it starts with your prayers.

> "So Jesus answered and said to them, 'Assuredly, I say to you, if you have the faith and do not doubt, you will not only do what was done to the fig tree, but also if you say to this mountain, Be removed and be cast into the sea, it will be done. And whatever things you ask in prayer, believing, you will receive" (Matthew 21:21-22 NKJ).

> "There is no one like the God of Israel, He rides across the heavens to help you, across the skies in majestic splendor. The eternal God is your refuge, and His everlasting arms are under you" (Deuteronomy 33:26-27 NLT).

3) Intercession is Standing in the Gap

> "If My people who are called by My name will humble themselves, and pray and seek My face, and turn from their wicked ways, then I will hear from heaven, and will forgive their sin and heal their land" (2 Chronicles 7:14 NKJ).

In the verse above the Hebrew the verb translated "pray" is defined as: "to intervene," or "to interpose," or "to judge." Here the Lord asked His people to intercede for others in their prayers. During the dedication of the temple, Solomon modeled intercessory prayer. He prayed to God on behalf of the people and continued in fervent prayer until the Lord answered.

"Now, my God, I pray, let Your eyes be open and let Your ears be attentive to the prayer made in this place" (2 Chronicles 6: 40 NKJ).

"When Solomon finished praying, fire came down from heaven and consumed the burnt offering and the sacrifices; and the glory of the Lord filled the temple" (2 Chronicles 7: 1 NKJ).

Intercessory prayer has been the catalyst that God honors to bring in revival and restoration.

Nehemiah prayed his way through rebuilding the entire city wall of Jerusalem in fifty days.

John the Baptist prayed, and thousands repented.

Paul prayed and changed the civilization of that era.

Moses prayed the Israelite nation out of Egyptian bondage.

Esther saved her people from certain death.

Abraham prayed for future generations—-that's you and me!!

4) We can Intercede by Reminding God of His Promises That are Yet to Be Fulfilled.

An example in scripture would be when Isaac interceded and prayed that God would give Rebekah a child. Isaac was forty-nine years old when he married Rebekah, and they waited twenty years for God to grant this prayer. And while

Rebekah experienced a season of infertility, as a result of prayer the Lord gave them two sons in the line of promise.

> "And the Lord said to her: 'Two nations are in your womb, two peoples shall be separated from your body; One people shall be stronger than the other, and the older shall serve the younger.' So when her days were fulfilled for her to give birth, indeed there were twins in her womb" (Genesis 25: 23-24 NKJ).

There are many promises in the Bible that are yet to be fulfilled. Take one that stirs your spirit and begin to proclaim it.

5) We can Intercede by Acting as an Advocate on behalf of Someone Else, Seeking God's Justice.
   This was demonstrated with Paul and Silas. When they were imprisoned unjustly, prayer went out and God answered. After an earthquake, the prison doors opened, and chains were loosed from prisoners, setting them free.

> "But at midnight Paul and Silas were praying and singing hymns to God, and the prisoners were listening to them. Suddenly, there was a great earthquake, so that the foundations of the prison were shaken; and immediately all the doors were opened and everyone's chains were loosed. And the keeper of the prison, awaking from sleep and seeing the prison doors open, supposing the prisoners had fled, drew his sword and was about to kill himself. But Paul called with a loud voice, saying, 'Do yourself no harm, for we are all here'" (Acts 16:25-28 NKJ).

I have personally experienced interceding for God's justice. I, along with others, have prayed to the Lord to position His people within government, and have seen a shift in both our provincial and federal governments. We have also prayed when someone has experienced injustice. When man's judicial system is not sufficient, seek God's justice.

Several years ago, my twelve-year-old son left for a two-week summer camp with the air cadets, his first extended time away from home. Needless to say, I was a little anxious. Several long hours later, I received a phone call from him telling me that another cadet was making threatening comments to him and a couple of other cadets. He asked me the meaning of some particularly explicit words, and I was immediately tempted to drive all night long to retrieve my son from the abuse of this juvenile delinquent! My son sounded traumatized, and I was a wreck! But when I went to the Lord with this matter, He reminded me that this trip was His idea and that much prayer had gone into it. I began to proclaim God's justice into the matter, praying that this would be a rewarding and maturing time and not a traumatic one for my son. After I went to God's throne room seeking His justice, the perpetrator was sent home and my son connected with a couple of other Christian boys and had a really good time. The only complaint he had was that drills and marches were painfully long and hot! But he learned many new skills and met some really great kids. God's justice prevailed!

An excellent resource on this area of intercession is an amazing teaching CD set by John Paul Jackson, entitled *Maximizing Heaven's Help*. I have listed other resources at the end of the book.

6) We can Intercede by Carrying the Burdens for Others

Jesus was the ultimate burden-bearer. He carried all our burdens and our sins to the cross.

Burden-bearing intercession is a specific type of intercession. Those who carry this gift can feel or sense what others are feeling. Examples of burden bearing can include "picking up" a certain feeling when entering a room, building, neighborhood, city, nation, etc. One can also "pick up" or sense something while in prayer. God can deposit a burden for someone or something, and that burden will create a strong desire, or even an urgency, to intercede. This type of intercession can last for a very specific time, or can last for months and years. Out of burden bearing can come our destiny.

I have a strong sense that there are many burden bearers out there. But without proper discipleship and discernment, burden bearers will walk around "owning" these feelings as if they were a part of their own personal make-up. This can produce feelings of depression and heaviness in these intercessors. I will speak to this situation further, in following chapters.

At times I have had a sensation when entering a place, and at other times I have been given very specific insight into a situation. God may give you words that have been plaguing a person and the feeling attached to them. Intercession can then be very direct, able to address the core problem in an instant.

One day when I was attending a church worship service several years ago, I heard certain such phrases as, "You don't belong here" and "You are not worthy to be in church." I immediately felt unworthy and wanted to leave that holy place. As I prayed for discernment, the Holy Spirit drew my attention to this new believer who stood nearby. I then began to intercede for him. I was standing between him and a satanic onslaught of lies that might have forever hindered his walk with the Lord.

"Bear one another's burdens, and so fulfill the law of Christ" (Galatians 6:2 NKJ).

7) We can Intercede for Spiritual Walls to Be Built and Strengthened or Torn Down in Order to Stand Against Satan.

"It shall come to pass, when they make a long blast with the ram's horn, and when you hear the sound of the trumpet, that all the people shall shout with a great shout; then the wall of the city will fall down flat. And the people shall go up every man straight before him. The Joshua the son of Nun called the priests and said to them, 'Take up the ark of the covenant, and let seven priests bear seven trumpets of rams' horns before the ark of the Lord.' And he said to the people, "Proceed, and march around the city, and let him who is armed advance before the ark of the Lord"' (Joshua 6:5-7 NKJ).

There are many walls, some that God has placed there, and some that need to be torn down. God's walls protect and provide a safe haven, such as a parent putting a gate up, so their toddler doesn't fall down the stairs. Satan's walls create division. A church I attended some years ago was in our "inner city" where theft and vandalism were high. Due to such problems, they ended up erecting a chain link fence with a locked gate. And while their heart is for the people in that community, the fence does not give an impression of welcome or warmth.

At the end of this book I will identify some terrific resources that have as their focus, intercession for cities, territories and nations.

8) As Intercessors We Represent the Needs of Another to God. We are His Ambassadors.

"Now then, we are ambassadors for Christ, as though God were pleading through us; we implore you on Christ's behalf, be reconciled to God" (2 Corinthians 5:20 NKJ).

In Dutch Sheets' book, *Beginner's Guide To Intercession*, he states, "Intercession will become a passion, not a performance, a lifestyle, not a labour."
We, as believers are all called to intercede, just as we are all called to prophesy.

"For you can all prophesy one by one, that all may learn and all may be encouraged" (1Corinthians 14:31 NKJ).

I strongly believe the two callings, prophecy and intercession, are linked. In order to prophesy, one needs to know what is on the heart of the Father, and intercession will bring you to a place of intimacy with Him, so that He may begin to speak to you. You and I certainly don't feel free to share our intimate thoughts and feelings with strangers or mere acquaintances, but save those things to share with dear friends. The same is true of our Father's relationship with us. There must be a level of comfort and intimacy on both sides before we can entrust each other with our deepest hopes and feelings.
Cindy Jacobs, founder and president of Generals of Intercession, states that: "All prophets are intercessors." She was taught that, "not all intercessors are prophets, but all prophets are intercessors." And if this is the case and there are unreleased intercessors, then there are also unreleased prophets! Prophets who are to speak divine words of healing and revelation to a lost and dying church as well as to a lost and dying world!

The following chapters are devoted to the two specific areas I want to address regarding intercession and you. Yes, you! I pray that the Lord will prepare you to receive His truth and that the doors to your destiny will be unlocked and thrown wide open. In Jesus' mighty name.

Chapter 3

Predestined for Intercession

I was pre-destined by God to be an intercessor, as are many of you. I was pre-destined to stand in the gap, to weep, to intercede for whomever God places upon my heart.

> "Before I formed you in the womb I knew you" (Jeremiah 1:5 NKJ).

My early years, my pre-Christian years did not resemble this priestly call in any way. In fact, quite the opposite was true. I have found that, more often than not, until God redeems the calling, the opposite will manifest itself. For example, someone with an anointing to teach may struggle academically, or someone with an anointing to prophesy will be misunderstood and struggle with rejection. The enemy does his best to sabotage prophetic words whether in the mind of the speaker or the receiver of the word. Prophetic words can bring life to someone or something that is dying.

> "Again He said to me, "Prophesy to these bones, and say to them, 'O dry bones, hear the word of the Lord! Thus says the Lord God to these bones: Surely I will

cause breath to enter into you, and you shall live" (Ezekiel 37: 4-5 NKJ).

"And then God said, "Let there be light;" and there was light. And God saw the light, that it was good; and God divided the light from the darkness" (Genesis 1:3 NKJ).

The spoken Word has always been powerful. God spoke creation into being. The same Spirit is in his children—in those who believe and confess Jesus as their Lord and Savior.

If the enemy can prevent the release of this amazing and powerful gift, then he has won that particular battle. I believe he has thwarted many prophetic words by deceiving people with respect to the gift of intercession and thereby shutting down prophecy, which can flow out of intercession. But we know that in the end victory is ours! Amen!

"And He said to me, 'It is done! I am the Alpha and the Omega, the Beginning and the End. I will give of the fountain of the water of life freely to him who thirsts. He who overcomes shall inherit all things, and I will be his God and he shall be My son'" (Revelation 21:6-7 NKJ).

As a child, I was an extreme introvert. I would go out of my way to stay out of the limelight. I didn't speak in school, even when asked a question. At recess, I would wait in line to go back inside; in fact, the less I had to interact the better. I would never make any eye contact. I looked at people's feet far more often than their faces. I knew who was in the room by their footwear! I found money on the ground on several occasions because my focus was always downward, not upward.

There was a two-fold explanation for this behavior. First of all I was very shy and felt terribly uncomfortable around anyone outside of my immediate family. Second, and more importantly, I could sense what others were feeling, whether good or bad (though usually it was bad). I was like a magnet for other peoples' emotions, but I didn't realize that not everyone was "wired" the way I was. Like most children, I believed my childhood experiences were the "norm," that everyone felt what I felt.

The greater the number of people around me, the more intense these feelings grew as I honed in on a wide range of intense feelings within a room. At times, this would become so overwhelming, so debilitating that I would need to leave. These emotions would most often be more negative ones including: hurt, pain, anger, guilt, shame, etc. I wasn't aware that these emotions belonged to others, and because they felt like mine, I would "own" them. It was a pretty scary world for a young child feeling many different and conflicting emotions with no rhyme or reason to explain them.

I was very susceptible to the environment around me. Television shows, movies, etc. would affect me much more they did others. I remember watching the Dick Van Dyke Show and feeling embarrassed for him when he would create some sort of a crisis. I couldn't watch frightening shows because they left me somewhat traumatized. I made the mistake of watching Alfred Hitchcock's *The Birds* and was so shaken that I didn't sleep at all that night (and neither did my sister, thanks to me). I also had several sleepless nights after that. My parents would simply describe me as being overly sensitive.

As an adult, I began to harden my heart, in order to survive. Eventually I was so shut off from my emotions that almost nothing impacted me.

"Therefore, as the Holy Spirit says: Today; if you will hear His voice, do not harden your hearts as in the rebellion, in the trial in the wilderness" (Hebrews 3: 7-8 NKJ).

When I received Jesus as my Savior, I wept for days and days and thought I would never stop. At one point I thought about buying stock in a facial tissue company! Now I realize that some of those tears were God healing my hardened heart and transforming it into a heart of flesh.

"Then I will give them one heart, and I will put a new spirit within them, and take the stony heart out of their flesh, and give them a heart of flesh" (Ezekiel 11:19 NKJ).

Some of those tears were for others; the intercessory cry and travail that had been shut down for years had suddenly been opened and was now overflowing.

Today, I still have tendencies to become either over-whelmed, picking up emotions around me or to shut down all together. The difference is that now I go to God with my needs and allow Him to direct me. He has taught me how to turn the intercessory burden over to Him and how to guard my heart appropriately.

"Be anxious for nothing, but in everything by prayer and supplication, with thanksgiving, let your requests be made known to God; and the peace of God, which surpasses all understanding, which guard yours and minds through Christ Jesus" (Philippians 4: 6-7 NKJ).

It's taken me a long time to get to where I am now. I will still retreat back to those old habitual ways of managing these circumstances but now I don't stay "stuck" there, burdened down or shut down for long. I recognize that it is about placing my trust in God and merely relying on Him for all things. After all, He is the one who created me this way! Perhaps He has created you in this fashion, too. I encourage you to ask Him right now.

From my earliest recollection, two themes played out over and over in my life. Fear and rejection. I now know that these were demonic assignments placed on me to prevent me from accomplishing my destiny. But we serve a huge God, and He is bigger than these demonic assignments. Amen!

Looking back, I can see Satan's hand on many aspects of my life. Because of the intuitiveness and discernment that accompanies the gifting, Satan could easily push me to feeling rejected and/or fearful. I received rejection on a daily basis. Little oversights were rejection for me. I was forgotten on many occasions because I was so shy and hidden. My very introverted tendencies made me an inviting target for the enemy.

I can recall a recurring dream where there would be a nest of snakes at the foot of my bed. If I moved my feet at all, I dreamt that I would be bitten and die. Awake or asleep, Satan had established control in my life.

I share this now because from this vantage point, I see how God used these circumstances to develop my character. I can persevere where before I would have given up. I recognize fear and rejection in others' lives and can speak freedom and truth. These childhood experiences were some of the building blocks for the intercessory gift. God is definitely in the restoration business!

"And God will wipe away every tear from their eyes; there shall be no more pain, for the former things have passed away" (Revelation 21:4 NKJ).

Here is the prayer of Nehemiah:

"I pray, Lord God of heaven, O great and awesome God, You who keep Your covenant and mercy with those who love You and observe Your commandments, please let Your ear be attentive and Your eyes open, that You may hear the prayer of Your servant which I pray before You now, day and night, for the children of Israel Your servants, and confess the sins of the children of Israel which we have sinned against You. Both my father's house and I have sinned. We have acted very corruptly against You, and have not kept the commandments, the statutes, nor the ordinances which You commanded Your servant Moses. Remember, I pray the word that You commanded Your servant Moses, saying If you are unfaithful, I will scatter you among the nations, but if you return to Me, and keep my commandments and do them, though some of you were cast out of the farthest part of the heavens, yet I will gather them from there, and bring them to the place which I have chosen as a dwelling for My name. Now these are Your servants and Your people, whom You have redeemed by Your great power, and by Your strong hand. O Lord, I pray, please let Your ear be attentive to the prayer of Your servant, and to the prayer of Your servants who desire to fear Your name; and let Your servant prosper this day, I pray, and grant him mercy in the sight of his man" (Nehemiah 1: 4-11 NKJ).

In the book of Nehemiah, the restoration of Jerusalem took place under the leadership of the prophet Nehemiah. In addition, scripture records a resulting revival and a repopulation of the city. God sent leaders and prophets to teach and guide the people into righteousness.

Chapter 4

Personality Profiles and Spiritual Inventories

In my journey to understanding the gift of intercession, I found it important to discover who I am, in all ways. I needed to know the difference between my soul and spirit. I needed to know the difference between my own woundedness and an intercessory cry in my heart. In this process I came across some personality profiles and spiritual inventories that I found very useful.

There are several personal profiles and inventories that are available online and or in books. The one I would recommend is by Florence Littauer. I have included her book in the resource section at the end of this book. In her book she describes four different personality types or profiles, including: (1) Sanguine, (2) Choleric, (3) Melancholy and (4) Phlegmatic.

As I went through the Personality Profile (which includes a list of forty questions and a score sheet) I discovered that I had primarily a melancholy temperament. This meant I am an introvert (no surprise there!) and a thinker. True to the profile I have a deep concern for other people and can easily be moved to tears of compassion. I am sensitive to the needs of others and can be very self-sacrificing. These are the strengths of a melancholy personality. These traits are God-given and are the makings of an intercessor!

I also discovered my weaknesses—I'm not lighthearted or much fun, but on the other hand a thoughtful melancholy disposition can be extremely helpful as an effective intercessor for God. On the down side I can also be moody and get easily depressed. I am often hesitant to begin new projects (like this book!). Through this exercise I learned that I have truly been pre-destined for intercession, but I can also quickly turn an intercessory gift into self-centeredness and deceive myself into believing it's all about me. I am completely dependent upon God for my daily needs and to speak truth. Everyday I need to check in with God for revelation and a tune-up! If I don't I can very quickly get to that place of self-centeredness where intercession becomes bottle-necked and useless.

Someone who has primarily a melancholy temperament would most likely be a "weeping" intercessor or a "feeling" intercessor. They would be quick to pick up other people's emotions and be able to "read" their surrounding environment. This temperament might be described by the secular world as "empathic" or on the downside, overly-sensitive.

The choleric is an extrovert and can be a very effective leader. Unlike the other personality types they are not easily discouraged and can stand in the gap for the long haul if God places a prayer burden that may not have immediate resolution. They are also able to stay optimistic throughout these long seasons. The choleric temperament has little need for friends, so their prayer life would not be dependent upon others. They can often be found leading intercessory prayer groups. This type of personality would make an excellent militant, warring intercessor, who makes prophetic decrees into the heavenlies!

On the downside, a choleric temperament may have some difficulty around the weeping intercessors. They may also have some problems with being under authority since they tend to want to be in control.

The sanguine temperament is also an extrovert. This individual can be very creative and has tremendous energy. They are wonderful encouragers and can bring hope and life to people and their situations. On the flip side, they can be undisciplined and have some difficulty finishing commitments. However, they can also be ground-breaking intercessors, taking new territory for the Lord.

My son is predominantly a sanguine temperament intermixed with some melancholy traits. He highly creative and is a wonderful encourager. He is destined to be an intercessor and a leader. At a very young age, he was discerning the environment around him. He also had a very tender heart for others. Although I think he's perfect (a mother's prerogative) he can wait until the eleventh hour to finish tasks.

The fourth temperament is described by the term phlegmatic. This temperament is introverted. Phlegmatics are watchers and have a very peaceful nature. They work well under pressure and can observe what is occurring in their neighborhoods, workplaces, cities and nations. The cry in their hearts will be for the Prince of Peace to come soon! A tendency toward laziness is what usually derails them from intercession.

All four personality types can be intercessors for the Lord. Each of us can typically display qualities of more than one type, but one temperament will usually emerge as dominant. I encourage you to discover who you are; a detailed study of the temperaments is one way to do this. In fact you may discover an amazing intercessory gift under the many layers of your personality! There are other profiles and inventories that you can explore as well. Some may focus on career paths and relationship strengths and weaknesses.

C. Peter Wagner has put together a very thorough inventory of spiritual giftings. In his book, *Your Spiritual Gifts*, he includes a comprehensive spiritual gifts questionnaire. Gifts of mercy, faith, discerning of spirits, knowledge, wisdom, prophecy, and exhortation may be giftings that would enhance intercession. He also includes the gift of intercession in his spiritual gift inventory. It is worthwhile to go through the inventory every couple of years or so, because when you begin to walk in your giftings, your score can change accordingly.

The reason I once again mention these resources is because it is our responsibility to discover who we are in Christ. We are all uniquely created, but, we all have a desire within us to discover both our identity and our destiny in the Lord, to see His vision expressed in our lives. I believe we are to take an active role in this process.

> "Not that I have already attained, or am already perfected, but I press on, that I may lay hold of that which Christ Jesus has also laid hold of me. Brethren, I do not count myself to have apprehended; but one thing I do, forgetting those things which are behind and reaching forward to those things which are ahead, I press toward the goal for the prize of the upward call of God in Christ Jesus" (Philippians 3:12-14 NKJ).

When my son was approximately ten years old, I bought him his first computer, and until that time I had no idea that God had gifted him in this area. During his summer vacation he took courses on basic computer repairs and other computer-related subjects to hone his skills. He now is gearing up for university in either computer science or engineering. We had absolutely no idea of this aptitude until it was revealed. Even as a Christian he needed to study and work to develop this gift; God didn't miraculously download all that he needed to know. In the same way the Apostle Paul encouraged the brethren to press on toward their goal—an ongoing process that takes time, effort and training.

I had no idea that I was an intercessor until I stepped into a few intercessory prayer groups and found myself connecting with others. I discovered a part of myself that, up to that point, was hidden. I then began to study this gift and press in toward the goal that God has placed before me. Intercession is truly an incredible hidden treasure within us.

Chapter 5

Qualities of Unreleased Intercessors

The following lists have been compiled from several intercessors I have known over the years. These "qualities" are meant to be used as a guideline only; they are not all inclusive, nor are they definitive. I merely hope to provide insight and to challenge previous conclusions you may hold regarding personality traits and begin to examine these traits through the eyes of intercession.

I have condensed the four personality types into two basic types; extroverts and introverts. Not all symptoms will speak to each reader; it is merely meant to provide some insight and perhaps, challenge some mindsets.

Type 1-Extroverts

These unreleased intercessors can have a strong tendency to be perfectionists. Even their greatest accomplishments fail to satisfy their high standards. As children and youth they may be excellent students, getting high grades, very task-centered. Their dissatisfaction is due to a non-awakened spiritual life and a desire for something more. They just don't know what that something more is, so they are always striving but without a sense of accomplishment or satisfaction. That something more is Jesus!

*Perfectionist (when walking with the Lord, this characteristic can be transformed into a gift of excellence)

*Overly busy—does not do well with quiet times, or down times. Will fill the void with activities, and as a result, they will have many acquaintances. Very few of these people will really know him/her. The perfectionist has a tendency to focus on works so as not having to look at character issues.

*Quick to see flaws in themselves and with others-without the Lord to soften their hearts and to discipline them these people can easily fall into judgments and criticism. Because of this, they may isolate themselves, even though they are extroverts and desire interaction with others.

*Prone to anger with varying degrees of outbursts. Because they have a strong desire to have order and, in their thinking, perfection, when this doesn't manifest itself in the world around them, they can express anger. This can manifest verbally as yelling, blaming others for the imperfections, or it can be physical to the point of assault.

These personality types are predestined to be administratively inclined. They make excellent organizational intercessors; praying for their church, ministry, community, etc. They may have prayer lists and will commit specific times to the Lord to spend in intercessory prayer. The extrovert in them may like to express the intercession through dance, song, or banners. They may also be more of a warring intercessor, very militant and strategic in their intercession. There is also a prophetic edge to them, which is tied into the dissatisfaction. They are not meant to be satisfied with the status quo; they are standing in the gap for what is to come, and calling it forth. But without Jesus in their lives, they are prone to bouts of frustration and angry outbursts, eventually becoming a toxic person to those closest to them.

Type 2—Introverts

With this type of personality, the person is very quiet and keeps their feelings hidden. As a child they can be left alone for extended hours at a time and may be seen as "the perfect child," never a problem. They will not do well in large gatherings of people until their confidence is built up through the Lord. Here are some possible traits:

*Shy, won't communicate unless necessary. They see and feel the world around them and take in more than they want. Although invisible, there will be a great deal of emotional turmoil going on underneath the surface.

*Unhappiness or depression will be common. Because they are like sponges for the emotional states of those around them, they will have many ebbs and flows with sorrow and depression. Not realizing they are picking up on the emotions of others, they will own these emotions as their own. They may be burden-bearing intercessors. And if this is so, they may be holding on to burdens that are not their own. Most likely, they will be doing this on an unconscious level.

*Very creative. These people will have a tendency to be drawn to creative things such as art, music, dance, etc. These outlets help them express the many facets of their emotions that otherwise go unexpressed. Without outlets for their creativity they will tend to find unhealthy ways to express themselves. This may open the door to substance abuse and other high risk behaviors.

These personality types may be predestined to intercede for others. They may be standing in the gap for lost loved ones, people who need healing or a miracle. They may be given a specific city or region to petition the Lord to come and transform. Their hearts may be stirred when they see someone in a wheelchair or someone in the hospital. Because of their quiet nature, they will pray for extended periods of time in solitude. Again, without having Jesus as Savior and Lord, this gift tends to look inward and often owns the pain around him. Something that was meant to be so precious to the Lord can actually be toxic to the individual, without Him.

As adults, both personality types will continue on their paths of unhappiness and despair; their unhealthy outlets will intensify. Until intercessors are plugged in to God and grow in understanding and wisdom regarding their destiny, they will continue to be unhappy and dissatisfied. Jesus is the answer, the only answer.

"Then Jesus said to them again, 'Most assuredly, I say to you, I am the door of the sheep. All who ever came before Me are thieves and robbers, but the sheep did not hear them. I am the door. If anyone enters by Me, he will be saved, and will go in and out and find pasture" (John 9:7-9 NKJ).

Chapter 6

Constipated Intercessors!

Until someone is released into the fullness of his calling as an intercessor he will still exhibit some of the same characteristics as the unreleased intercessor. I call these people *constipated intercessors*! They recognize the gift and are walking in the calling, but only in part. They may have received healing from past hurts and be able to move into healthier relationships and choices, but there will still be some residue left in their spirit that is unfulfilled. This will create a tendency to revert back to those familiar patterns of behavior. Also, when they are interceding, it may not be as pure as it can be, but will be a mix of intercession and some personal/soul issues. The problem is these intercessors may also go on to be constipated prophets! And if that is the case the prophetic gift will not be pure, either. R. Loren Sandford writes an incredible book entitled *Purifying the Prophetic*. In it, he states that "The blood of Jesus is everything to the Christian. Without His character imparted through His death in and through His blood, we can never truly live."

In addition to some of the qualities previously mentioned, condemnation may also be added to the mix. As Christians, we can fall into condemnation when we lack understanding and wisdom. Again, we have the possibility of "owning" these intercessory burdens and cries in our hearts, making for some very weighted down Christians (hence the term *constipated*).

> "Come to Me, all you who labour and are heavy laden, and I will give you rest. Take My yoke upon you and learn from Me, for I am gentle and lowly in heart, and you will find rest for your souls. For My yoke is easy and My burden is light" (Matthew 11:28-30 NKJ).

I can't tell you how many times I have attempted to rebuke and renounce an intercessory burden, thinking the enemy was attacking me. I am sure he is alright with taking the credit, if it prevents us from fulfilling our destiny. Likewise, I have taken the credit for something on an emotional level that was in reality an intercessory burden. If we don't grow in wisdom, we will stay unreleased (or in prison) and deceived. Satan's trump card is always deception and he wins *only* when we believe the deception.

> "that their hearts may be encouraged, being knit together in love, and attaining to all riches of the full assurance of understanding, to the knowledge of the mystery of God, both of the Father and of Christ, in whom are hidden all the treasures of wisdom and understanding" (Galatians 2:2&3 NKJ).

Further, Christians may be more inclined to hide from others, reluctant to share what is going on if it is negative. We sometimes get the notion that we should be all healed, completed restored and share only good news. And the longer we're Christians the more entrenched this stronghold can become. That notion is another lie from Satan, one that often prevents us from coming into our destiny, but no more! Declare your freedom! The house of cards is falling!

I was an addictions counselor working with male adult offenders for more than a decade. During that time my pastor approached me, asking if I would be willing to offer an addictions counseling/program for the people in the church. I initially thought, "Wow! This is going to be great and easier than my usual clientele." What I discovered was that it was far more difficult. A defensive wall went up in many of the church people, a mental stronghold that prevented some badly needed healing. On the other hand, the offenders were more up front about their problems. With the Christian group, a façade was present though I don't believe it was deliberate. But that's how Satan works; he gets you to "own" the garbage, which allows him greater access into your life. I daily ask for wisdom to be an offensive warrior, rather than a defensive one. When I look back I can see where I had allowed Satan to strategize and win against me far too often.

Here's another example. Several years ago, I was at a Vineyard conference in Winnipeg, Manitoba. (That's in Canada just in case this book reaches other countries) At the time, the church was being pastored by David Ruis. At one point in the conference, during some awesome, anointed worship, I was totally undone by the Holy Spirit.

Years later I still ponder what took place. I was traveling with three friends, one of whom was the woman who led me to Christ and discipled me in those early years. During this particular service she stood on my left and placed her hand on my back Long after she removed it I could still feel a hand on my back. It was the Holy Spirit! A powerful impartation was released. This was an impartation for intercession. I didn't know this at the time, but things were never going to be the same for me again! Praise God!

Moments later, the church was filled with the joy of the Lord, and people were laughing and shouting praises unto the King! I was not; instead I was crying uncontrollably from deep inside! A cry from my belly. This went on throughout the duration of the weekend regardless of what God was doing around me. I was weeping and travailing. (At the time, I didn't know what travail was....until I came across books by Cindy Jacobs and James Goll).

Interestingly enough the woman God used to release the impartation was not an intercessor, or so she said at the time. In fact she was adamant that she was not an intercessor, but she was definitely moving prophetically. How could someone be prophetic and not be an intercessor? I saw a link between the two gifts even back then. Today, however, she admits that she is, and she moves very powerfully in intercession.

This experience raised a few questions in my mind. First, here was a very grounded woman of God who was leading people to Christ and discipling them, but who did not discern her gift of intercession. It took several years to bring about the change in her thinking and in her heart. Did Satan deceive her? Or was God's timing the issue? Was her heart not ready to receive the calling of an intercessor? In fact, it was probably a mix all these things. But what really got me going was that if my spiritual mom (who I consider very grounded in her faith) could not see the intercessory gift how many others in the church are in this same boat? This question stayed with me and in the end became the impetus for this book. I would become fired up in my spirit (okay, an intercessory burden!) that these people need to be released into their destiny. The scripture God gave me in the midst of these questions was this:

"Deep calls unto deep at the noise of your waterfalls; all your waves and billows have gone over me" (Psalm 42:7 NKJ).

Deep within the recesses of my spirit, He was speaking to me. I could not understand the specifics of His "speech," yet I knew it was Him and I knew it would change my life forever.

Over the years, I would have similar encounters with other people. Some were Christians and some were not. I would see, hear or sense an anointing for intercession, yet these people were oblivious to the call.

"Where there is no revelation, the people cast off restraint; but happy is he who keeps the law" (Proverbs 29:18 NKJ).

In this verse the Hebrew word for revelation is defined as a revelatory vision, a word from God. Without God's revelatory word, His people will perish. We require His revelation in order to thrive.

"And it shall come to pass in the last days, says God, that I will pour out of My Spirit on all flesh; your sons and your daughters shall prophesy, your young men shall see visions, your old men shall dream dreams. And on My menservants and on My maidservants I will pour out My Spirit in those days, and they shall prophesy" (Acts 2: 17 & 18 NKJ).

Soul Vs. Spirit

Time and time again, I have come across many Christians who don't grasp the clear distinction between the spirit and the soul. When asked, they will admit there is a difference because the Word of God defines them as two separate and distinct parts of man. Understanding the difference is critical in understanding intercession, but it is also difficult. The gift of intercession is a spiritual gift. Our burdens, feelings of sorrow or sadness can be a result of an intercessory gift, or they may result from something festering in the soul. Our soul can interpret situations and the environment around us, and our thoughts and emotions can respond. So it's clear we need to interpret correctly where "our feelings" are coming from—our soul or our spirit.

> "For the Word that God speaks is alive and full of power (making it active, operative, energizing, and effective); it is sharper than any two-edged sword, penetrating to the dividing line of the breath of life (soul) and (the immortal) spirit, and joints and marrow (of the deepest parts of our nature), exposing and sifting and analyzing and judging the very thoughts and purposes of the heart" (Hebrews 4:12 Amplified).

I have been extremely blessed to have received an excellent teaching by John Paul Jackson. In his course, *The Art of Hearing God*, offered through Streams Ministries, he clearly teaches the differences. John Paul Jackson states, "The soul is comprised of the 1) mind, 2) will and 3) emotions. As we mature spiritually, there is a continued breaking of the soul and a corresponding increase in your spirit. If you are not led by the spirit, you will be led by the soul. In 1 Corinthians 2:10 we are told that the Spirit reveals the deep things of God to those who have 'received the Spirit who is from God.' A thick, hard soul will trap and not allow the release of the spirit. If the soul is not broken, it will be hard to consistently hear God."

John Paul Jackson goes on to teach that the spirit is comprised of 1) wisdom, 2) conscience, and 3) communion. He further states that "a choice must be determined as to whether a man's spirit or soul will prevail." If your spirit isn't ruling in your life your soul is in command.

An example of my soul in control would be if I chose to stay home from work, school or church because on an emotional level, I felt like being lazy and wanted to sleep in.

An example of my spirit leading would be: despite my desire to sleep in, I know that laziness is not from God and I am a person of integrity who gets up and gets busy. Sometimes, unfortunately, the distinction is just not that clear cut. The decision you have to make appears to be a good one. Perhaps it's a job offer. I've been taught by Rick Joyner that what appears "good" may not be God. Again, Satan's tactic is to deceive. As we mature in Christ, the choice won't be to discern between what is evil and what is good, it will be to discern what is good and what is God.

Putting all of this into a context for an intercessor is invaluable. When God makes a deposit into your spirit, you need to intercede. An intercessory cry is not the same as soul issues stemming from offenses and woundedness, either from past experiences (your own past or generationally) or from present day situations. These are areas of your soul that need healing. I have discovered that once I have received a healing in a particular area, God will frequently deposit it into my spirit—now as a burden to pray on behalf of others.

"But you, beloved, building yourselves up on your most holy faith, praying in the Holy Spirit, keep yourselves in the love of God, looking for the mercy of our Lord Jesus Christ unto eternal life. And on some have compassion, making a distinction" (Jude 20-22 NKJ).

Just as in the natural, a recovered alcoholic (as the world puts it; I don't like the word alcoholic) becomes an addictions counselor or a cancer survivor works in a cancer clinic—in the spiritual realm the same thing occurs.

"The kingdom of heaven is at hand. Heal the sick, cleanse the lepers, raise the dead, cast out demons. Freely you have received, freely give" (Matthew 10: 8 NKJ).

Where God has healed us and set us free, we have an anointing to give that healing away to others.

What we do with these experiences is critical. We have a choice to move from a position of hurting and requiring prayer and healing, to a position of wholeness where we can intercede for others. Because God uses all things to teach us and heal us, we need to be continually in a place where we are asking Him to lead and bring revelation in every situation.

I would like to pray right now for you. Lord, I ask that You would bring understanding to readers regarding soul versus spirit. We need to grow in wisdom in all matters. Lord, I ask that You would release revelation and that clarity would come. Lord, may anything that is contrary to Your Word would fall off each one. In Jesus' name. Amen.

Burden Bearing

Once more, I point you to some of the incredible teachings and resources available today. The Sandfords (John and Paula) have taught significantly in this area. Eddie and Alice Smith have also authored great teachings.

One type of intercession is burden bearing. This is where an intercessor can truly identify with the person(s) they are upholding in prayer. If a person praying is unaware that he or she is an intercessor, in that particular situation they will most likely presume that their response is an emotional one and further believe it is all about them. They will take something that God deposited into their spirit and transfer it into their soul and "own" it. Here is where it is critical to get into the Word of God. He alone can expose what is soul and what is spirit.

> "For the word of God is living and powerful, and sharper than any two-edged sword, piercing even to the division of soul and spirit, and of joints and marrow, and is a discerner of the thoughts and intents of the heart" (Hebrews 4:12 NKJ).

With burden bearing, God desires us to release an intercessory cry, sent up to Him. We are to partner with Him. But when we end up presuming this is our baggage we can become depressed, frustrated and even angry, weighted down and ineffective, in our own lives and on behalf of those God wants us to impact. If this happens we will respond out of our soul instead of our spirit, and it won't be pretty! Believe me, I know!

The Sandfords teach on this subject, and I would encourage those who feel they are burden-bearers to seek out these resources. They further teach on burden-bearing defilement and how those called into this type of ministry will need to be cleansed spiritually so they do not become defiled as they stand in the gap.

On one occasion, I was a vessel God used in deliverance. I was standing in the gap for someone for their freedom from much demonic activity. At the time, I felt it was a privilege to be used by the Lord, which it is. But I wasn't aware of needing to be cleansed from any defilement. After the event I had disturbing dreams and felt almost depressed. I was also unable to hear from the Lord with any clarity. I felt that somehow my peace had been stolen. When I received a teaching regarding cleansing prayers after such intercession and then received ministry, I sensed an immediate freedom and the peace of God returned! Amen!

I wonder how many intercessors are shut down spiritually as well as physically as a result of similar situations. These situations can even occur while the intercessor is completely unaware that he is bearing another's burden. The following is a list of some potential symptoms of one who has been defiled from burden bearing:

1) You may not be as intimate with the Lord as you once were
2) You may be easily distracted
3) You may spend less time in worship and in prayer
4) You may have physical symptoms ranging from sleeplessness to sleeping too much
5) Other physical symptoms may include feeling exhausted or out-of- sorts (My son describes this feeling as being a "little off").
6) You may, subconsciously, pull away from those with the gift of discernment
7) Overall, your peace has been stolen. This will most likely happen on such a slow, insidious level that you may be unaware for a period of time. This will also make it more difficult to identify the source of the attack.
8) Your ability to hear from God may be affected. You may not get a clear sense of direction.
9) You may receive "demonic attacks" primarily with your thinking.

If you identify yourself in the above list, it may be as a result of burden bearing defilement. If so, you need to be cleansed by the Holy Spirit. You may also need to repent if you have carried burdens that you were not meant to carry, or that you were not meant to carry past a specific time or season. As intercessors, it can be very difficult to release things to the Lord, but it is critical. The battle is the Lord's.

We are merely vessels. This is probably one of the most difficult things for me to do. I know I have tendency to hang on longer than God wants, especially if the situation has not yet been completely resolved. For example, if God placed a burden to pray for someone's salvation and he is not yet saved, I'll want to hang onto the burden until I see him come to salvation, but that may not be God's plan for me. He may have placed the burden on me for a season and may release it and place it on someone else and have something else for me. Again, it goes back to daily dependence upon God and checking in with Him. When I have over-extended myself in intercession, it will be in my own strength, and His grace will have lifted. I will then feel exhausted, out- of-sorts, and can easily slip into depression and isolation. These symptoms prove that I have been led by my soul and not by my spirit. This is not fun at all!

Lord, for those who are burden bearers, I offer a prayer of deep healing. If they have been defiled by carrying burdens that were not from You, or longer than You intended, cleanse them. I plead the blood of Jesus over them body, soul and spirit. For those who have been shut down and hurt, bring complete restoration. I pray a blessing over them and the burdens You have given them. I ask that You would bring clarity so they know the difference. In Jesus' name. Amen.

Character is Always More Important than Gifting

There is another awesome teaching from John Paul Jackson's course, entitled *The Art of Hearing From God.* He states that "Character determines whether someone actually reaches his/her destiny. Character is defined as emotional, intellectual, and moral qualities; moral or ethical strength." Character carries the weight of the gifting. God wants to pour out power, and it is by His grace that He withholds it because our character could not handle the fullness of His unleashed power. The reality is that we are the only ones that will keep us from God's call and destiny on our lives. Saul couldn't prevent David from fulfilling his destiny. In fact, God even factored David's character flaws into his destiny. He has done the same for you and me! Amen!

"The foundation of a person's life is built on the results of choices that are made from birth. This determines one's eternal destiny." This is another awesome nugget from John Paul Jackson!

"Therefore whoever hears these sayings of Mine, and does them, I will liken him to a wise man who built his house on the rock: and the rain descended, the floods came, and the winds blew and beat on that house; and it did not fall, for it was founded on the rock. But everyone who hears these sayings of Mine, and does not do them, will be like a foolish man who built his house on the sand: and the rain descended, the floods came, and the winds blew and beat on that house; and it fell. And great was its fall" (Matthew 7:24-27 NKJ).

"Every good gift and every perfect gift is from above, and comes down from the Father of lights, with whom there is no variation or shadow of turning" (James 1:17 NKJ).

"For I am the Lord, I do not change..." (Malachi 3:6 NKJ).

"One thing I have desired of the Lord, that I will seek: that I may dwell in the house of the Lord all the days of my life, to behold the beauty of the Lord, and to inquire in His temple, When You said, 'Seek my face,' My heart said to You, 'Your face, Lord, I will seek" (Psalm 27:4,8 NKJ).

Chapter 7

But God...I'm not an Intercessor—I'm just Depressed!

I don't know how many times I have heard these words or something similar. And for the most part it was women who spoke them. (Don't feel neglected, men, the next chapter may be for you). When we confuse what is spirit with what is soul, we will end up with the wrong diagnosis.

Several years ago, I had incredibly severe pain in my right shoulder blade area. It would persist for several hours and was extremely debilitating. This went on for years because doctors never accurately diagnosed the cause. Finally, I learned the correct diagnosis. The problem was my gall bladder, and I was experiencing referred pain, which made the diagnosis quite difficult. It wasn't until I learned the correct diagnosis that I received the appropriate treatment and could heal. This is also true of the diagnosis of emotional pain, whether of soul or spirit.

If the soul, which involves our intellect and emotions, is operating, then sadness or a state of depression can result after intercession. If our spirit is taking the lead and we feel grieved, though it is not merely our personal own sadness or depression, it is still a matter God needs to address.

I believe a couple of things can occur in this instance. Emotions resulting from intercession often aren't properly addressed because people believe it is simply an emotional state and "own" the feelings. The enemy loves this, because it effectively takes out an intercessor as well as stalling the intercession. And then, eventually, the intercessory burden which is in our spirit will impact our soul and threaten our emotional well-being. Just as an untreated infection will affect other areas of our body, so will an "untreated" intercessory wound in our spirit!

I'm not saying that all depression is the result of an intercessory prayer burden, but I am would be willing to bet that a large number of people who struggle with persistent feelings of unhappiness, constant dissatisfaction, and depression are not walking out their destiny as intercessors.

1) Symptoms of depression:

A depressed mood—feeling "sad" or "hopeless" or "empty" or "in despair" or they may cry frequently. Children and adolescents may also exhibit irritability and anxiety.

A diminished interest in or potential to experience pleasure, from most normal daily activities

Sleep disturbances-insomnia or sleeping too much

Weight changes-significant changes in weight when not attempting to gain or lose—a gain or loss of 5% or more in a month

Exhaustion-deep fatigue or a loss of energy

Feelings of worthlessness or guilt, or feeling overwhelmed by life

Difficulty making decisions

Thoughts of suicide or death

Physical aches and pains

Restlessness

Loneliness and isolation

The medical profession does not have a clear understanding of why people experience depression. Most believe it is a complex "disease" that can develop for a variety of reasons. It can affect anyone of any age, gender, race ethnicity or income level. Sometimes, its onset occurs after a major life change (such as the death of a loved one or a divorce), but small events seem to trigger depression as well.

The medical profession believes that the mind and body are linked. How we feel emotionally has an affect on how we feel physically. Doctors recognize that emotions can influence the body to release certain hormones that trigger diseases, including but not limited to cardiovascular disease, allergies, autoimmune diseases, cancer and heart disease.

According to the American Institute of Stress any where from 75- 90% of all visits to primary care physicians are the result of stress-related disorders. So the scientific link has been made between body and soul (emotions, will and intellect). The next step is to recognize the link with our spirit. We are tripartite beings consisting of body, soul and spirit.

"Now may the God of peace Himself sanctify you completely; and may your whole spirit, soul and body be preserved blameless at the coming of our Lord Jesus Christ" (1Thessalonians 5:23 NKJ).

John and Paula Sandford write:

"Sometimes depression mysteriously lifts, seemingly unaccountably. One wonders who may have been pumping the handle of prayer unseen and unknown, whether some chemical lack or imbalance was suddenly overcome, or whether the Lord, who moves in mysterious ways, simply sent a ray of light. For whatever reason, depression sometimes slowly or suddenly unaccountably departs, but the point is that the depressive had nothing to do with it and knows he didn't. Overcoming depression is not a matter of willpower." (7)

2) The following is a list of symptoms of those who are gifted as burden-bearers and prophets:

R. Loren Sandford developed an amazing profile of a prophetic person:

"We come in all sizes and shapes, some of us serious in nature and some of us loving a good joke, some intellectual and others having no education at all. But at heart, we are very much alike in many respects.

<u>Rarely happy</u>- Burden-bearing

"Prophetic people are rarely "happy" people- at least until they have served long and made peace with the gift, with the pain of the burden and with God. For a prophetic person, training involves depths of crushing and breaking that seem incomprehensible to the average Christian…..this training period and the heaviness of spirit that may accompany it can last for many years. This heaviness need not be permanent. Seasoned prophetic people who have persevered over time seeking the presence and the heart of heart of God and who have allowed suffering to effect the character changes it was intended to produce come at last into a deep abiding peace and joy that are not easily shaken. One source of the dark moodiness that so plagues some prophetic types, therefore, is the pressure of the constant seasons of crucifixion required to produce the character adjustments that are so essential to the calling.
Burden bearing is one of the most difficult aspects of prophetic awareness to sort out and balance…..Not all

burden bearers are prophetic, but all prophetic people are burden bearers. We deeply feel everything going on in the hearts of people around us."

Sandford continues; "I finally fell into a clinical depression and remained there for many years, although I continued to function as a pastor, husband and father. Several attempts at counselling led nowhere, having run aground on the failure of my counsellors to understand what they were dealing with, not to mention my own blockheaded rigidity.

At last, at the perfect time in my life and in the plan of God, I met a healing couple whose tools and level of compassion were just the right stuff. With their help God granted release and freedom where locked up feelings were concerned, not just in the area of burden bearing but in my entire emotional life. Everyone connected with me benefited, beginning with my family. Prophetically gifted people need differently gifted people for balance, healing and wholeness.

Months after that wonderful release, I found myself once again overwhelmed. Waves of paranoia, fear and despair that I knew had no root in my own life threatened to sweep me away, but this time the outcome was different. Good counselling had at last connected me with the Father's love at a level I had never known, so that as I sought the Lord in prayer, He did something new with me. I share it here as a visual representation of the scriptural command in 1 Peter 5:6-7,

> "Therefore humble yourselves under the mighty hand of God, that He may exalt you at the right time, casting all your anxiety on Him, because He cares for you."

As I prayed, I suddenly felt as if I were standing under and inside the mouth of the tornado of the Holy Spirit swirling all around me. This inverted funnel served as a great vortex drawing the paranoia, fear and despair out of the people of my church and up through to the Lord.

After what must have been about thirty minutes of this form of resting in the Spirit and letting the swirling funnel do its work, I fell into a state of peace. Better than this, I was filled with a clean, rested and holy love for the people of my church that I had not felt in a very long time."

There seems to be some similarities with R. Loren Sandford's experiences of a burden bearer and prophet and of depression. Let's go on with Loren Sandford's profile:

Regarding "The gift of weakness"- he states: "While every believer responding to the call to discipleship must live this life of the cross, it must go deeper for the prophetic person, and so there are constant blows to pride and ego and to elements of character that do not yet resonate the character of Jesus. Sometimes this aspect of the heavy hand of God sends me into seasons of heaviness, but mostly at this stage of my life I can welcome it in gratitude and go on with joy undisturbed. 'A rebuke goes deeper into one who has understanding than a hundred blows into a fool.' (Proverbs 17:10) "Faithful are the wounds of a friend, but deceitful are the kisses of an enemy." (Proverbs 27:6). And what a friend I have in Jesus!

But this life of humbling and breaking can cause the prophetic person, especially the immature and unseasoned one, to appear to be constantly unhappy." (Does this sound like depression?!!)

"Eccentric personalities- Prophetic types are usually eccentric personalities who have experienced more than their share of rejection because they do not think, feel or even act like other people.. Not only are they misunderstood by others—even by their families and intimate loved ones— but they are seldom understood even by themselves. Like so many things prophetic people face internally, this lack of self-understanding diminishes with maturity and healing, but I do not know of a prophetic person who has not experienced it.

Self-protections-Many a burden-bearing child with prophetic gifts becomes the family scapegoat, the repository of everything the other family members cannot face or express. Instinctively, brothers and sisters—and parents as well—project their pain onto the moody one, often acting it out with ridicule and torment until a root of rejection takes hold that shapes life and pollutes perceptions."

Loneliness and isolation- "Because of this lack of common perspective, people sometimes have trouble relating as friends and peers, while we, in turn, have trouble relating to them.....

Prophetic people live as forerunners. They are usually one step ahead of the rest of the Body of Christ. When other people are down and out, the prophetic person may already be rejoicing in the blessing to come. Or when others catch up and find the joy and blessing the prophet saw coming, the prophet has already moved on and now grieves over a failure and apostasy that will form the essence of the coming days." (8)

Loren Sandford goes on to identify other characteristics including: uncommon experiences, awareness deficits, rejection, or being overly serious about life, as well as a history of life-threatening events.

Examples in the Bible include King David who struggled with depression and was an intercessor.

"My heart is severely pained within me, And the terrors of death have fallen upon me, fearfulness and trembling have come upon me, and horror has overwhelmed me" (Psalm 55:4-5 NKJ).

Elijah also battled depression. He too, was an intercessor and prophet.

"But he himself went a day's journey into the wilderness, and came and sat down under a broom tree. And he prayed that he might die, and said, 'It is enough! Now, Lord, take my life, for I am no better than my fathers!'" (1Kings 19:4 NKJ)

I don't want to leave you with the impression that all depression is unreleased intercession or that everyone with a depressive disorder is an intercessor just needing to tap in to the Holy Spirit. What I am saying is that some of the depression that people carry is not really depression but an intercessory burden whether they believe they are an intercessor or not. It will be up to you and your journey with God to discover your gifting and the calling He has on your life. Lord, I pray right now that You will reveal giftings and callings to Your people. Your word says that without vision, your people perish. We don't want to perish, but rather we want to thrive and grow. We want to mature to fulfill our destinies. In Jesus' name. Amen.

Chapter 7

But God, I'm not an Intercessor...I'm just Angry!

I have also come across many people whose anger has been a "righteous anger" that, as with some depressed individuals, has been an intercessory burden that did not get released to the Lord.

There is a strong link between injustice and anger. And God is definitely into justice!

> "Of the increase of His government and peace there will be no end, upon the throne of David and over His kingdom, to order it and establish it with judgment and justice from that time forward, even forever. The zeal of the Lord of hosts will perform this" (Isaiah 9:7).

We don't have to look too far to see injustice. It exists in our own communities, in our governments, courts, schools, and yes, even the church. When we walk things out in our soul, we can become angry at all the injustices we see each day. When we walk things out in our spirit we are stirred up to cry out to the Lord to move in these areas.

I have also met people who were angry and it wasn't "righteous" anger, and sometimes not even rational. They were just angry! Well, it still could be unreleased intercession. I was told once that my frustration was a result of intercessory prayers not released. As I pondered this, I could see how frustration could easily turn into anger if it is left to fester. I know I can get frustrated when I don't pray daily unto the Lord.

I have taught anger management to some very angry men for over a decade. Most of their angry was a result of unmet expectations. Whether it was in a relationship or even with themselves, each had a desire that was unmet. For many of these men, it was an accumulation of unmet desires over a period of many years. As a Christian, I know all my desires will be met as my relationship with God grows.

> "Trust in the Lord, and do good; Dwell in the land, and feed on His faithfulness. Delight yourself also in the Lord, and He shall give you the desires of your heart" (Psalm 37:3-4 NKJ).

So what is God waiting for? He is waiting for us to turn our hearts to Him, so He is, then, justified to act on our behalf! Amen!

> "Therefore the Lord will wait, the He may gracious to you; and therefore He will be exalted, the He may have mercy on you. For the Lord is a God of justice; blessed are all those who wait for Him" (Isaiah 30:18).

Many of our emotions have an anger component to them. Depression and fear can be linked to anger. Some of the research in the area of our emotions indicates that anger is a secondary emotion. Behind the scenes is an even stronger emotion. Generally speaking, men will gravitate towards anger whereas women predominantly turn things inward with depression.

So, are you an angry person? Do you get easily frustrated when things don't go the way you planned? Do you get annoyed by other people's negative behaviors? What about when you are stuck in traffic, others are late for appointments, you are lied to, or you receive faulty merchandise? What about when you fail to get what you are entitled to? There are anger inventories such as the Navoco Anger Scale that can give you some insight into anger. If you answered yes to the some of the questions above, I would encourage you to take the inventory.

There is a great deal of study and research linking anger to physical illnesses and diseases.

Psychiatric diseases have been linked to unresolved stress, anxiety and anger. Anxiety disorders, panic attacks, post-traumatic stress disorder, obsessive compulsive disorders and phobias can also be associated with these emotions.

Physical problems are also connected to anger and stress. The list is long. It includes heart and vascular issues, gastro-intestinal problems, headaches, pain and inflammation, skin conditions, genitourinary tract problems, allergies, and immune deficiencies.

All evidence supports that one needs to get to the root cause or the source of the anger in order to heal. What if that root cause is an intercessory cry? It would stand to reason, then, that all other attempts to heal and get set free from anger, including forgiveness, would not bring complete healing to the sufferer. If this sounds like you, perhaps your anger is related to intercession. Intercession can look like anger when we are crying out for justice. But there is a difference between a righteous anger and unrighteous anger. The emotion of anger is a godly one if used in the spirit.

For example Jesus became angry and overturned the money-changers' tables in the temple.

> "Then Jesus went into the temple of God and drove
> out all those who bought and sold in the temple, and
> overturned the tables of the money changers and the
> seats of those who sold doves. And He said to them,
> "It is written, My house shall be a house of prayer,
> but you have made it a den of thieves" (Matthew
> 21:12&13 NKJ).

If you're angry due to an injustice, freedom will come through prayer and intercession. Many intercessors cry out daily for laws to be changed, for leaders to be led by God, and for specific people groups and nations. Sometimes these intercessory injustices have been rooted in an injustice that has happened to us or to a loved one (the loss of a child, abuse, family or personal substance abuse issues, etc.). In these cases, healing and forgiveness need to occur before a pure intercessory cry can take place.

Several years ago I spent some time helping out in a street ministry and was particularly impressed with a woman who would come in twice a week and drop off sandwiches for the children. She was in her 70s and a devout intercessor. Her cry (one of them) was for the young girls who had become prostitutes. Her prayer life and volunteerism reflected this. Another individual there also had a heart for the children due to her past experience with abuse and being on the streets. This experience produced an intercessory burden for others. Unfortunately, because this last individual was still in need of healing, her initial attempts at ministry were disastrous. In the end, God's timing is everything. He is concerned with both our healing and our character. That doesn't necessarily mean that we sit on the sidelines until we are totally restored, but we need to hear from God as we step out into ministry.

Many leaders believe their house has to be in complete order before they step out into ministry. But when we submit to Him, He will work out the timing and show us the way. Amen.

Part Two

Getting Started and Staying Connected

Chapter 9

Individual Prayers and Exercises

Probably the most helpful piece of information that I could pass on, is that God really wants you to grow in wisdom in the area of prayer and intercession. It is not His intention to leave His children in the dark,, wondering what is our "soul issues" and what is our "spirit issues". So our job is to continually seek Him and ask of Him. When in doubt, ask God what is going on. In time, you will discern His voice and therefore will be able to discern between soul and spirit. Your daily prayers need to include asking God to show you and to teach you how to pray.

A second piece of invaluable information is the following: prayers and intercession are vertical forms of communication. This means that our conversations are going up, towards the throne room. Prayers and intercession are not horizontal form of communication, meaning we don't talk about God has revealed to you about someone to others. The fastest way I know of to shut things down in the intercessory realm is to share (gossip) what God is revealing in your prayer time with others.

There is a difference between seeking godly counsel and disclosing private information. If you are uncertain if sharing information is godly counsel, best to err on the side of staying silent. God will direct you and provide you with the counsel you require. He will never place a task on your plate without the resources to complete it.

Daniel 9 is definitely one of intercession. Here Daniel is praying for repentance for Israel's past transgressions, but it was also a prayer of proclamation for God was about to overthrow the Babylonians and the Jews were to return to their homeland.

"Then I set my face toward the Lord God to make request by prayer and supplications, with fasting, sackcloth, and ashes. And I prayed to the Lord my God, and made confession, and said, "O Lord, great and awesome God, who keeps His covenant and mercy with those who love Him, and with those who keep His commandments, we have sinned and committed iniquity, we have done wickedly and rebelled, even by departing from Your precepts and Your judgements. Neither have we heeded Your servants the prophets, who spoke in Your name to our kings and our princes, to our fathers and all the people of the land. O Lord, righteousness belongs to You, but to us shame of face, as it is this day—to the men of Judah, to the inhabitants of Jerusalem and all Israel, those near and those far off in all the countries to which You have driven them, because of the unfaithfulness which they have committed against You.

O Lord, to us belongs shame of face, to our kings, our princes, and our fathers, because we have sinned against You. To the Lord our God belong mercy and forgiveness, though we have rebelled against Him. We have not obeyed the voice of the Lord our God, to walk in His laws, which He set before us by His servants the prophets. Yes, all Israel has transgressed Your law, and has departed so as not to obey Your voice; therefore the curse and oath written in the Law of Moses the servant of God have been poured out on us, because we have sinned against Him. And He has confirmed His words, which He spoke against us and against our judges who judged us, by bringing upon us a great disaster, for under the whole heaven such has never been done as what has been done to Jerusalem.

As it is written in the Law of Moses, all this disaster has come upon us; yet we have not made our prayer before the Lord our God, that we might turn from our iniquities and understand Your truth."(Daniel 9:3-13 NKJ).

We can follow Daniel's example. Daniel began by turning to God. Turning to the Lord indicates that we are turning away from something; the world, our fleshly desires or Satan. Daniel then submitted himself to the Lord. He recognized His power and authority as well as His holiness. Daniel praised Him and acknowledged His character of love and sovereignty. Next, Daniel acknowledged the truth about his position and proclaimed his confidence in God having the answer to his prayer. Daniel prayed with anticipation.

Another intercessory prayer is the prayer of binding and loosing. We can bind something on earth if it doesn't take place in heaven and we can loose something that we don't see on earth, but exists in heaven.

"And I will give you the keys to the kingdom of heaven, and whatever you bind on earth will be bound in heaven, and whatever you loose on earth will be loosed in heaven." (Matthew 16:19 NKJ).

Another discipline we can establish for our prayer life is to spend time in His presence. Terms such as soaking or to wait upon the Lord have been used to describe this practice. Getting quiet and begin to open your heart to the Lord is the beginning of soaking. Invite Him to search your heart and ask to receive more of Him. Give the Holy Spirit permission to work in your heart. This can be a part of your daily regime with the Lord.

> "He gives power to the weak, and to those who have not might He increases strength. Even the youth shall faint and be weary, and the young men shall utterly fall, but those who wait upon the Lord shall renew their strength; they shall mount up with wings like eagles. They shall run and not be weary. They shall walk and not faint." (Isaiah 40:29-31 NKJ).

Chapter 10

Finding the Right Intercessory Group

Just as you need to find the right church it's important to find an intercessory prayer group where you can fit in and grow up into your destiny.

Personally I tend to feel like someone is trying to suffocate me when I get put on a prayer list and people call me to pray for Aunt Sue's gall bladder or Harry's trip to Mexico. I am equally shut down when there is a structured format that dictates ten minutes of praying in tongues for the leadership, and so on. This is just my personal preference and how I am put together. Others enjoy these formats and the structure. I pray that God will bless those who intercede, going before God to advocate for the needs of others.

Then there's the group that is more inclined to war in the spirit. There may be warring by dance, shouts, declarations, etc. There are intercessory groups who do spiritual mapping and are focused on geographical cleansings and taking back the land. There are different streams of the Holy Spirit and there are different streams and functions within the intercessors themselves. No matter what your preference it will be helpful to connect with like-minded intercessors. You will be able to press in and intercede for longer durations when necessary, when all intercessors are on the same page. If you are in the right church there's a good chance there will be intercessors who have a similar burden to your own. You may have different personalities and different expressions of the Holy Spirit but your hearts will knit together to establish unity and release the kingdom of God into the areas for which God has burdened you. Ask God to reveal other intercessors to you within your church. Perhaps it's not your church but your workplace. I believe every workplace is a place of missions and ministry. Again, ask God to reveal the intercessors He wants you to connect with. There can also be other intercessors in your community or neighborhood, or your school or your children's school, etc. Ask God, and if He has placed the burden on your heart it is very likely that He has placed the same burden on others. Don't look with your natural eyes, but with the eyes of your spirit, because some of these intercessors may still be hidden, unreleased!

SMALL GROUP STUDY GUIDE

1) Leadership Information

The following is a list of some biblical characteristics of a leader:

1. Availability-

There is no sense starting something that you can't put your heart into. It will mean some preparation time with practical tasks and in prayer. It will also demand an ongoing commitment.

2. Good Listeners-

Leaders and intercessors need to have an ear to God. To pray only what you hear from the Lord. All intercession begins in heaven, where Jesus is interceding at the Father's right hand.

"Therefore he is able to save completely those who come to God through Him, because He always lives to intercede for them" (Hebrews 7:25).

3. Faithfulness and Trustworthiness-

"His master said to him, Well done, you upright (honourable, admirable) and faithful servant! You have been faithful and trustworthy over a little; I will put you in charge of much. Enter into and share the joy (the delight, the blessedness) which your master enjoys" (Matthew 25:23 Amplified).

4. Transparency, walking in integrity and honesty-

This is true for all leaders. When you are leading an intercessory prayer group, you are dealing with matters that are very close to God's heart. These issues are not meant for everyone to hear. Sharing something that should be held in confidence could do significant damage.

5. A Servant's heart-

"And going into the house, they saw the Child with Mary His mother, and they fell down and worshipped Him. Then opening their treasure bags, they presented to Him gifts- gold, frankincense and myrrh" (Matthew 2:11NKJ).

"And Jesus called them to Him and said, You know that the rulers of the Gentiles lord it over them, and their great men hold them in subjection. Not so shall it be among you; but whoever wishes to be great among you must be your servant, and whoever desires to be first among you must be your slave- Just as the Son of Man came not to be waited on but serve, and to give His life as a ransom for many (the price paid to set them free)" (Matthew 20:25-28 Amplified).

6. An Attitude of Submission-

"For I also am a man subject to authority, with soldiers subject to me. And I say to one, Go, and he goes, and to another, Come, and

he comes; and to my slave, Do this, and he does this" (Matthew 8:9 NKJ).

7. Under Authority-

I would strongly encourage intercessors to be under authority before starting an intercessory prayer group. If all members are from one church, it will simply mean approaching your pastor and sharing what God has placed on your heart and what you would like to do. Having your pastor bless and release you puts you under proper authority and covering. If members are from different churches, then the onus is on them to speak to their pastors. As leader(s) you will need to go to your pastor(s) and come under their authority. If this isn't done, it just opens the door to offense and lack of covering. God will make a way if it is His will. He will never give you a burden and a task, and then not supply the resources to accomplish it.

> "Now a centurion had a bond servant who was held in honour and highly valued by him, who was sick and at the point of death. And when the centurion heard of Jesus, he sent some Jewish elders to Him, requesting Him to come and make his bond servant well. And when they reached Jesus, they begged Him earnestly, saying, He is worthy that You should do this for him, for he loves our nation and he built us our synagogue. And Jesus went with them. But when He was not far from the house, the centurion sent friends to Him, saying Lord, do not trouble for I am not sufficiently worthy to have You come under

my roof; neither did I consider myself worthy to come to You. But speak a word, and my servant boy will be healed. For I am also a man subject to authority, with soldiers under me. And I say to one, Go and he goes; and to my bond servant, Do this and he does it. Now when Jesus heard this, he marvelled at him, and He turned and said to the crowd that followed Him, I tell you, not even in Israel have I found such great faith" (Luke 7:2-9 NKJ).

8. Release of Authority-

Relationship with God is critical. It is impossible to operate in the power and authority of God if don't have a relationship with Him. We need to be able to know what He is saying and doing. John Paul Jackson defined spiritual listening as "quite distinctive from simple listening. Spiritual listening requires that we focus and listen for the benefit of other person."
We also will need a measure of faith.

"But to as many as did receive and welcome Him, He gave authority(power, privilege, right) to become the children of God, that is, to those who believe in (adhere to, trust in, and rely on) His name" (John 1:12 Amplified).

We need to walk in obedience to the Holy Spirit. This may mean taking risks, maybe to the point of appearing foolish to others.

"So Samuel said: Has the Lord as great delight in burnt offerings and sacrifices, as in obeying the voice of the Lord? Behold, to obey is better than sacrifice, and to heed than the fat of rams" (2 Samuel 15:22 NKJ).

Here Samuel was emphasizing that an attitude of sincerity and obedience were prerequisites for worship that pleased God.

9. Responsibilities of a Leader-

The primary responsibility of the leader is to facilitate the move of the Holy Spirit. We are to be instruments (I love the word "conduit") to release God's love, healing, impartations, and whatever He wants to do! To lead, in God's kingdom, means to serve, and to give of ourselves.

Always seek the Lord first. As a leader, you will need to discern what people are bringing forward. Something may not be from the Lord, and may be merely someone's personal agenda. Or it may be from the Lord, but out of season. It will the leader's job to seek God and ask of Him. He will show you what and when He wants done.

10. Leadership in pairs-

Solomon, a very wise leader, knew the power that was released in partnering.

"Though one may be overpowered, two can defend themselves. A cord of three strands is not quickly broken" (Ecclesiastes 4:12 NKJ).

There are two types of partnerships identified in Matthew 18. First we have a partnership when people come together to pray, and secondly, we become His partner when the Holy Spirit shows up.

> "Again I say to you that if two of you agree on earth concerning anything that they ask, it will be done for them by My Father in heaven. For where two or three are gather together in My name, I am there in the midst of them" (Matthew 18: 19 NKJ).

11. Fasting and Intercession-

When fasting is coupled with intercession there is an incredible potential for spiritual power and answered prayers. We are not to seek the spiritual power; rather we are to seek the Lord. Jesus himself fasted for forty days.

> "Jesus, full of the Holy Spirit, returned from the Jordan and was led by the Spirit into the desert, where for forty days he was tempted by the devil. He ate nothing during those days, and at the end of them he was hungry" (Luke 4:1 NKJ).

Fasting combined with intercession can build faith, bring spiritual breakthroughs, and increase discernment and humility.

2). <u>General Guidelines for an Intercessory Group Format</u>-

> "And the dragon stood before the woman who was ready to give birth, to devour her Child as soon as it was born. She bore a male Child who was to rule all nations with a rod of iron. And her Child was caught

up to God and His throne. Then the woman fled into the wilderness, where she has a place prepared by God, that they should feed her there one thousand two hundred and sixty days" (Revelation 12: 4-6 NKJ).

The above scripture speaks to me of intercession. Intercession is all about crying out in order to birth something that exists in heaven and desiring "it" to manifest itself on earth. Satan will want to devour the intercessory prayers. It's also true that not every place will be a safe place to intercede.

I recall a time when a friend (another intercessor) and I visited a new ministry in a nearby city. We had been invited there as intercessors to pray for the ministry. We were in the sanctuary doing just that, and suddenly I felt shut down and defiled. Someone had entered the sanctuary carrying a demonic spirit that thwarted our intercessory prayers in an instant.

We now pray against any demonic influences and take an offensive posture. We also ask the Lord where He wants us to go. As we've seen, not every place will be safe. Understanding your authority and where God has called you will be critical to effective intercession.

Use the following only as general guidelines. You don't want to "box" God in or restrict Him in any way.

1. Length of time- Two to three hours is generally long enough, but don't confine the Holy Spirit to a time frame; sometimes it may be longer. This is especially true once your group becomes established and working in unity,
2. Leader(s) will need to prepare the environment. The room will need to be comfortable. If people like to lie down, blankets and cushions might be a nice touch.

Bibles, paper and pens should be available to people. Having a room free from distractions is important. Make sure there are: no phones or if there is a phone, turn off the ringer; no young children, babies or animals, etc. You may want to have maps and/or a globe, and a bulletin board or an easel, somewhere to post and track prayer requests, photos and promises from God.

3. Leader(s) should get together prior to each intercessory prayer time. Allow a minimum of thirty minutes before each session to pray and cleanse the environment. If the place you are using is used for several different purposes, then you may want to consider praying longer in preparation.

4. Leader(s) may want to spend the first session(s) doing some teaching on intercession and how the prayer times will flow. You may have "veteran" intercessors, but not when it comes to an intercessory prayer group. Otherwise you may get people with prayer lists and requests, or people who will engage on a "social" level, wanting to fellowship and simply visit. Some people aren't used to waiting on the Lord for any length of time, and this could cause anxiety or discomfort.

5. Encourage people to be on time, otherwise latecomers will be a distraction. You may want to lock the door or leave a note on the door indicating the there is a prayer group in session and you would prefer not to be disturbed.

6. You may have a closed group, not allowing for any new members. If your direction from the Lord is for a specific purpose of for a specific season, a closed group may be the way to go. You may have an open group to encourage growth and new groups to be birthed out of the original group. If the latter is

the case, you would want leaders-in-training to be trained and equipped to start a group of their own. In addition, you may want to stagger the new people so that unity and relationships are established. Also, you can do a brief teaching in sessions where new people first attend. This could be a function for the leaders-in-training.

7. Journaling requests is a great way to record all that God reveals as well as all that God does. Going through your journals and seeing all the answered prayers will really boost your faith and encourage people to press in to Him.

8. A cleansing prayer should include the following:

A)-To remove any desecration. Destroy or remove any articles that are not holy unto the Lord.

B)-Cleanse the area in prayer. "In the power and authority of Jesus Christ, I command any evil thing that inhabits this space for any reason to leave right now. I command that all rights and grounds that have been given to the kingdom of darkness be broken immediately. I command that any associated curses or incantations be broken now. All this I do in the power and authority of the Lord Jesus Christ."

C)-Consecrate and dedicate the location to the Lord.

"I dedicate this place to you, Lord. I ask that You would cleanse this place by your Holy Spirit and set your seal upon it. I ask that You pour the blood of Jesus Christ over this place and make it impervious to the kingdom of darkness. I ask that Your glory would shine and that Your name would be glorified. Please station your holy angels to protect this place.

I pray this all in the name of the Lord Jesus Christ. Amen."

D)-Anoint the space.

"Lord, I ask that You bind all evil in the air, the ground and water. Satan and all evil, you are bound. I plead the blood of Jesus Christ, protecting those who enter into this place, our loved ones, our possessions, and everything in or on it. We break every satanic dedication now in the name of Jesus Christ. We seal this place in the blood of Jesus Christ. Amen."

E)-Maintain protection.
Pray over the place for cleansing and protection every time you use it for intercession. This is really critical, especially if the space is used by others, for other purposes.

3) <u>The intercessory prayer time format</u>:

1. A brief prayer inviting the Holy Spirit to have His way! Pray that each person would have ears to hear and eyes to see what God wants for the time together.
2. A brief time of worship, to bring people into His presence and allow them to focus on Him. Instrumental or soaking music can be left on through the time if it helps people to stay in His presence.
3. Waiting upon the Lord. This can be anywhere from twenty minutes or longer. If this is a new group, twenty minutes may seem like a very long time. This is a discipline that may need to be encouraged.

"Be still and rest in the Lord; wait for Him" (Psalm 37:7 NKJ).

"Wait and hope for and expect the Lord; be brave and of good courage and let your heart be stout and enduring. Yes, wait for and hope for and expect the Lord" (Psalm 27:14 NKJ).

4. Ask the group what the Lord has revealed to them. This could be a picture, a scripture, a person, an event, a place, etc. Leaders may want to go first, in the beginning, to give the group a sense of things. The one who has an intercessory revelation is usually the best person to pray, because the anointing will most likely lie on that person. The others will come alongside and lift that person in prayer, standing in agreement.
5. Allow sufficient time for all to share each revelation from the Lord.
6. Depending upon the group and what God has laid on your hearts, you may also want to minister to the people within the group. If so, it's best to do this at the end. This type of prayer group is to hear from God and intercede according to what God reveals. This may or may not include personal ministry.
7. Always close in prayer. You will want to seal what has been interceded for and bless the members. If there was any type of deliverance or spiritual warfare, a cleansing prayer would be appropriate and to pray against any defilement.

4 Journaling Examples-

A basic example might look like the following:

Date: people in attendance prayers/scripture date answered

....
....
....

Another example:

Date: ....

Who was involved:

The situation presented; both physical and spiritual aspects:

The scriptures that support the issue, and how God has dealt with a similar situation in scripture:

The prayer:

The outcome:

----

5) <u>Possible Hindrances</u>-

   1. Lack of Faith

> "Who do men say that I, the Son of Man, am?"
> So they said, "Some say John the Baptist, some
> Elijah, and others Jeremiah or one of the prophets.
> He said to them, "But who do you say I am?"
> Simon Peter answered and said, "You are the
> Christ, the Son of the living God." Jesus answered
> and said to him, "Blessed are you, Simon, Bar-
> Jonah, for flesh and blood has not revealed this to
> you, but My Father who is in heaven. And I also
> say to you that you are Peter, and on this rock
> I will build My church, and the gates of Hades
> shall not prevail against it. And I will give you
> the keys of the kingdom of heaven, and what-
> ever you bind on earth, will be bound in heaven,

and whatever you loose on earth will be loosed in heaven" (Matthew 16:14-19 NKJ).

"Them He arose and rebuked the wind, and said to the sea, "Peace, be still!" And the wind ceased and there was a great calm. But He said to them, "Why are you so fearful? How is it that you have no faith? And they feared exceedingly, and said to one another, "Who can this be, that even the wind and the sea obey Him!" (Mark 4:39&40 NKJ)

2. Not God's plan

"You ask and you do not receive, because you ask amiss, that you may spend it on your pleasures" (James 4:3 NKJ).

Sometimes we pray for the wrong things. At the time it may appear to be both God's will and the right thing to pray. We need to remember we only see in part—He doesn't give us the entire picture. But when we are persistent in prayer we will discover His will and He will direct us.

I can recall crying out to the Lord, very fervently, to release me from a practicum placement in which I was working. It was disturbing me on both a soul and spirit level. I sought out the leaders in my church to stand with me in this prayer, but they did not!! Fortunately, they were wise in their response and told me that it might not be God's plan to release me. They were correct; God had some things for me to do there. In fact, I was privileged to be able to lead several people to the Lord! Shortly after that, I was released, six weeks before my actual contract ended. Due to my personal emotional struggle I wasn't seeing the entire picture.

3. Unconfessed sin can prevent God from answering prayers.

"Confess your trespasses to one another, and pray for one another, that you may be healed. The effective, fervent prayer of a righteous man avails much. Elijah was a man with a nature like ours, and he prayed earnestly that it would not rain, and it did not rain in the land for three years and six months. And he prayed again, and the heaven gave rain, and the earth produced its fruit" (James 5:16 NKJ).

4. Lack of unity

"I, therefore, the prisoner of the Lord, beseech you to walk worthy of the calling with which you were called, with all lowliness and gentleness, with longsuffering, bearing with one another in love, endeavoring to keep the unity of the Spirit in the bond of peace. There is one body and one Spirit, just as you were called in one hope of your calling, one Lord, one Faith, one baptism, one God and Father of all, who is above all, and through all, and in you all" (Ephesians 4:1-6 NKJ).

Unfortunately, I have been in many prayer groups where there has not been unity. Even in small groups, there can be offenses that are not reconciled or differing opinions not handled in a godly manner.

Ideally, it is best to address these matters quickly before the offense brings division.

In one instance two people (both gifted intercessors) allowed an offense to come between them over a book. One intercessor borrowed a book from the other and then subsequently lost the book. This situation did not get resolved early enough and the offense became a wedge in their relationship.

5. Unbelief

"Jesus said to him, "If you can believe, all things are possible to him who believes." Immediately the father of the child cried out and said with tears, "Lord, I believe, help my unbelief" (Mark 9:23&24 NKJ).

6. Timing

"Then the Lord answered me and said: "Write the vision and make it plain on tablets, that he may run who reads it. For the vision is yet for an appointed time; but at the end it will speak, and it will not lie. Though it tarries, wait for it; because it will surely come, it will not tarry" (Habakkuk 2:2-3 NKJ).

7. Warring in the heavens

"Then he said to me, 'Do not fear, Daniel, for from the first day that you set your heart to understand, and to humble yourself before your God, your words were heard; and I have come because of your words. But the prince of Persia withstood me twenty-one days; and behold, Michael, one of the chief princes, came to help me, for I had been left alone there with the kings of Persia" (Daniel 10:12-13 NKJ).

Sometimes we forget that there is a spiritual aspect to what we are attempting to enter in for. God has given me glimpses into the intense warfare that goes on when His children pray. I love Frank Peretti's books such as *This Present Darkness* that describes the ongoing exchange between what we see with our natural eyes and what goes on in the heavens. Although his books are fiction, I believe God gave him tremendous revelation.

Part 3

From Intercession to Prophecy!

PROPHETIC INTERCESSION

"But if they are prophets, and if the word of the Lord is with them, let them make intercession to the Lord of hosts, that the vessels which are left in the house of the Lord, in the house of the King of Judah, and at Jerusalem, do not go to Babylon" (Jeremiah 27:18 NKJ).

L et's look at how we move from intercession to prophecy. If, in your intercession you are praying and standing in the gap for things that are yet to be fulfilled or are not presently evident, then your prayers are prophetic in nature.

In Cindy Jacobs' book, *The Voice of God*, she writes the following:

"Intercession is the training ground for the prophetic gifts. I personally believe that almost all prophetic intercessors have the ability to prophesy on a regular basis or to become prophets. As I write later on about the various kinds of prophets, we will see that they may prophesy in song, or as they counsel or minister in front of a congregation. Prophets vary in nature, and therefore do not all use the same prophetic vehicle to prophesy.

As intercessors begin to experience regular answers to their prayers from supernatural knowledge given to them by God, many step forward to share with someone else what they are sensing. I like to mentor young prophetic believers by taking them with me as I travel and having them pray with me. They often become very excited and say, "Cindy, I knew what you were going to pray before it came out of your mouth!" the same Holy Spirit praying through me was also praying through them."(9)

John Loren Sandford, in his book, *Elijah Among Us,* states:

"Intercessory prayer is both a function of prophets and a major task. Prophets are essential to the work of end time intercession. Not only are prophets themselves to intercede, but the Body of Christ needs to know the specifics of when and what to pray about." (10)

John and Paula Sandford write in *The Elijah Task*:

"In addition, intercessor-prophets are frequently aware that sin is a corporate matter, that they share in the guilt of the one for whom they pray. Otherwise they offer prayers from a lofty rather than a lowly position, which will never work since God draws near to the humble and contrite (Isa. 57-15). (11)

In James Goll's book, *Kneeling on the Promises*, he states:

"Revelatory giftings of God, I am convinced, are for the many, not just the few. The Lord is looking for an entire generation of passionate people (called the Church!) who will walk in the spirit of wisdom and revelation in the knowledge of the Lord Jesus Christ.
What does it mean to be part of a company of prophetic people? God wants each of us to stay so close to His heart so that we can speak a relevant word from Him in a contemporary manner into different

echelons of society. We are called not only to stand up in a church meeting and speak out a prophetic word, but to be world-changers, history-makers and Kingdom-builders by taking revelatory gifts—the prophetic presence of the Holy Spirit—out into the spheres of influence the Lord has appointed for us.

Don't just get a word; become a word for Jesus' sake! Be a contemporary sign from God that will make people wonder what is going on. Let them watch your life and remark, "God must be alive and well on planet earth!""(12)

My heart is to see James Goll's statements become a reality in my own life as well as the life of my church. The church should be seen as different from the rest of the world, because of Christ in us, flowing out of us. Becoming prophetic should impact the world around you, affecting your loved ones and your sphere(s) of influence.

In Mike Bickle's book, *Growing in the Prophetic*, he identifies four different levels of the prophetic gift. The first level he identifies as 1) simple prophetic. This type of prophecy is one of encouragement, comfort and exhortation (1 Corinthians 14:3). The second level he describes as 2) prophetic gifting. Here, the person gets regular revelation from God. They may not always have the interpretation to the revelation. The next level is 3) prophetic ministry. Bickle sees this level as those whose gifting has been recognized for regular ministry in the local church and are able to interpret most of the revelations they get from God. The last level, he identifies as 4) prophetic office. Here, the individual operates in signs and wonders and can prophesy with 100% accuracy. He notes that they are not infallible.

I strongly believe that moving from intercession to prophecy involves developing an intimate relationship with

God. It is impossible to speak out God's heart, if you do not know Him.

I am far better at discerning what is going on in my son's life and what is in his heart than I am a mere acquaintance. The closer we are to someone the easier it becomes to know what is in their heart. This is true of our relationship with God. I especially admire prophets like Bobby Connor or Dick Mills. They have so much of the Word of God in them. Prophecies they give are saturated with scripture. These men ooze scripture!! This can only come from time spent studying the Word and spending time in His presence daily!

T. Austin Sparks describes prophetic ministry as spiritual interpretation. He states in his book, *Prophetic Ministry*,

> "It is the interpretation of everything from a spiritual standpoint; the bringing of the spiritual implications of things, past, present and future, before the people of God, and giving them to understand the significance of things in their spiritual value and meaning. That was and is the essence of prophetic ministry."(13)

No wonder Satan wants a foothold in intercession and prophetic giftings. When there is freedom for intercession and prophecy, the church will finally become the powerhouse it is meant to be!

In R. Loren Sandford's book, *Understanding Prophetic People*, he writes the following:

> "Prophetic people tend to gravitate toward intercessory ministry because the calling inevitably draws them there. This is as it should be. If most prophetic people must remain hidden, then what they hear from God falls into the category of guidance for prayer. The chief role of prophetic people intercessory groups is

to receive revelation concerning direction for prayer. In fact, one key calling for prophetic people is cry out to God on behalf of others on the basis of prophetic revelation and guidance. Although this revelation and guidance comes from heaven, earthbound pastoral guidance remains essential." (14)

I strongly agree with Sandford's comments. Several years ago, I had a small group of women over to my house on a weekly basis. We were learning to hear from God and began to move into intercessory prayers for our loved ones and workplaces. The group disbanded for several reasons; the primary reason was that God's agenda was complete— at least, in that format. A few months later, some of the women wanted to re-start the group and approached me. I prayed about it but didn't get clearance from God. One of the concerns I had was that these women were from another church and I wanted a blessing from their pastor before stepping back into the role of leading this group. They then moved the group to another location and continued on with a slightly different agenda. During this time frame, some of the women experienced difficulties within their church and subsequently left the church (not on a positive note).

I have learned the hard way that the need for pastoral guidance is essential. Groups that went well, without any huge setbacks all had pastors or leaders overseeing the group. My pastor was aware of what I was doing; he was apprised on the direction of the intercession, and would bless and pray for us. Some of the intercessory groups kept a journal and allowed my pastor access to it. God is into unity and acknowledging godly authority.

Another aspect of growing from intercession to prophecy is a point at which God will deal will our character. Several years ago, I was taught that Christians will inevitably go through a wilderness season or what others describe as "the dark night of the soul." It seems that we are usually given a season of being wrapped up in our Father's arms; we feel His love, our prayers get answered and being His child is, by far, the best thing in the universe. Then, one day, things are different. We cry out to the Lord and it's as if He not answering. We may still feel His presence, but that "totally saturated" feeling isn't there as much as before. Life situations seem strained; relationships, finances, family, health, work, and school are just some areas where we are taking a beating, and things become difficult to say the least. We cry out, "God, where are You? It's me — remember me, the apple of Your eye?" This season is especially true for intercessors and prophets. The early successes and answers to our prayers allow us to build a confidence (in us - I can do this; He is in me!) and a faith in Him (He is alive, all things are possible!). The wilderness season is a time to address our character and allow God to pluck out what would prevent us from moving forward and going deeper with Him.

R. Loren Sandford describes the wilderness sojourn and the dark night of the soul as two different journeys. He describes the wilderness as a time that strongholds of self must be broken, the flesh is crucified, and unbelief is rooted out. He states that everyone bearing a prophetic destiny will go through a wilderness. The dark night of the soul is deeper still. Sandford writes," The higher the calling, the deeper the hole required for the foundation." In his book, *Understanding Prophetic People,* he writes that "the dark night brings about cross-centered, compelling compassion." This training is all about our character development. In fact, I wonder how many people resist the "training" at some point, and the end result is dissatisfaction. Living in that place of dissatisfaction can bring about depression and/or anger if we stay there long enough. Just as unforgiveness can produce bitterness and a hardened heart, resisting training can also produce similar issues of the soul. The process may not be pleasant, and it inevitably lasts longer than we would like, but the end result is awesome! It is exactly what we have been destined for! And one of the incredible attributes of our heavenly Father is that He always desires to give us another opportunity to re-align ourselves with our destiny. Satan knew our destiny before we did, and he sets in motion many strategic plans to de-rail us. It can begin before we were born. But, ultimately, it is our choice. We can choose to be led by our spirit and not our soul. Yes, it's a lifelong process. We can ask God to expose the lies and examine ourselves as the Holy Spirit sheds His glorious light on us. We can look at what we have seen as our emotional make-up of sadness, hurt, depression or anger and frustration and allow God to bring revelation and truth. We can ask for discernment and His judgment regarding our heart. We can say yes to finishing the race and not stopping halfway, because it became too difficult, too lonely, or too uncomfortable.

I know that at times I have left when things got tough. In the short term, it is easier. But I realize now, I have been created for the long term; it's called eternal life! Short term would have me leave church or a relationship if there was an offense. It's easy. Short term would have me let my soul lead and satisfy an emotional hurt by avoidance or shutting down. But, I'm crying out for my spirit to lead and for my soul to follow. I cry out for the Spirit of the Lord to lead me in all areas, big and small.

I think of Job and everything he went through. Restoration and abundance came, only after he repented and began praying for his friends. Wow! That sounds like intercession to me!

"And the Lord restored Job's losses **when** he prayed for his friends. Indeed the Lord gave Job twice as much as he had before" (Job 42: 10 NKJ).

Do you want to finish the race? Do you want God to bring restoration and blessings in your life? Do you want God to realign you so that you do? It is the only thing that will bring you sustained joy. It's what you were created for!!

"Bear one another's burdens, and so fulfill the law of Christ" (Galatians 6:2 NKJ)

"Now may the God of hope fill you with all joy and peace in believing, that you may abound in hope by the power of the Holy Spirit" (Romans 15:13 NKJ).

Awesome Resources

Intercession/ Prayer

Books-

Bickle, Mike with Hiebert, Deborah, *The Seven Longings of the Human Heart* (Kansas City, Missouri: Forerunner Books, 2006).

Campbell, Wesley and Stacey, *Praying the Bible* (Ventura, California, Regal Books, 2002).

Chavda, Mahesh, *The Hidden Power of Prayer and Fasting* (Shippensburg, PA.: Destiny Image Publishers, Inc., 1998).

Christenson, Larry, *The Mantle of Esther* (Grand Rapids, MI.: Chosen Books, 2008) **

Cooke, Graham, *Developing Your Prophetic Gifting* (Sovereign World, 1994).

Cymbala, Jim, *Breakthrough Prayer* (Grand Rapids, MI: Zondervan, 2003).

Damazio, Frank, *Seasons of Intercession* (Portland, Oregon: BT Publishing, 1998).

Frangipane, Francis, *The Place of Immunity* (Cedar Rapids, IA: Arrow Publications, 1994).

Frangipane, Francis, *The Power of Covenant Prayer* (Lake Mary, Florida, Charisma House, 1998).

Goll, James, *Kneeling on God's Promises* (Grand Rapids, MI: Chosen Books, Baker Book House Company, 1999). **

Grubb, Norman, *Rees Howell's Intercessor* (Fort Washington, Pennsylvania, 1975).

Hall, Dudley, *Incense and Thunder* (Sisters, Oregon: Multnomah Publishers, Inc., 1999).

Jacobs, Cindy, *Possessing the Gates of the Enemy* (Grand Rapids, MI: Chosen Books, 1991).

Johnson, Bill, *Strengthen Yourself in the Lord* (Shippensburg, PA.: Destiny Image Publishers, Inc., 2007). **

Johnson, Bill, *When Heaven Invades Earth* (Shippensburg, PA.: Treasure House, an imprint of Destiny Image Publishers, Inc., 2003). **

Murray, Andrew, *Andrew Murray on Prayer* (New Kensington, PA: Whitaker House, 1998).

Murray, Andrew, *The Secret of Intercession* (Springdale, PA: Whitaker House, 1995).

Pierce, Chuck D. and Dickson John, *The Worship Warrior* (Ventura, Calif., Regal Books, 2002). **

Pierce, Chuck D. and Wagner Systema, Rebecca, *Prayers that Outwit the Enemy* (Ventura, Calif., Regal Books from Gospel Light, 2004). **

Sheets, Dutch, *The Beginner's Guide to Intercession* (Ann Arbor, MI.: Servant Publications, 2001).

Sheets, Dutch, and Ford III, William, *History Makers* (Ventura, Calif.: Regal Books, 2004)

Sheets, Dutch and Jackson, Chris, *Praying Through Sorrows* (Shippensburg, PA: Destiny Image, Publishers, Inc., 2005).

Smith, Eddie, *Help! I'm Married to an Intercessor* (Ventura, Calif., Renew Books, a division of Gospel Light, 1998).

Smith, Eddie and Hennen, Michael L., *Strategic Prayer, Applying the Power of Targeted Prayer* (Grand Rapids, MI: Bethany House Publishers, 2007).

Terhune, Lila, *Cross Pollination* (Shippensburg, PA.: Revival Press an imprint of Destiny Image Publishers Inc., 1998).

Wiedrick, Dennis, *A Royal Priesthood* (Canada: The Master's Foundation, Wiedrick and Associates, 1997).

Yonggi Chou, David, *Prayer that Brings Revival* (Lake Mary, Florida, Creation House, Strang Communications Company, 1998).

CDs-

Johnson, Bill, *Filled with the Fullness of God* (Redding, Calif., Bill Johnson Ministries)

Johnson, Bill, Prayer: The Kind That Changes the World (Redding, Calif., Bill Johnson Ministries) **

Holy Spirit

Books-

Davis, Paul Keith, *Thrones of Our Soul* (Lake Mary, Florida: Creation House, 2003).

Hinn, Benny, *Good Morning, Holy Spirit* (Nashville, Tennessee: Thomas Nelson, Inc., Publishers, 1990).

Hinn, Benny, *The Anointing* (Nashville, Tennessee: Thomas Nelson, Inc., Publishers, 1992).

Jacobs, Cindy, *The Supernatural Life* (Ventura, Calif.: Regal Books, 2005). **

Johnson, Bill, *Face to Face with God* (Lake Mary, Florida: Charisma House, 2007).

Keefauver, Larry, *Experiencing the Holy Spirit* (Nashville, Tennessee: Thomas Nelson, Inc., 2000).

Kuglin, Robert J., *Handbook on the Holy Spirit* (Camp Hill, PA.: Christian Publications, 1983).

Sheets, Dutch, *The River of God* (Ventura, Calif.: Renew Books from Gospel Light, 1998).

CDs-

Jackson, John Paul, *Relationship with the Holy Spirit* (North Sutton, NH: Streams Ministries International) **

Prankard, Rev. Bill, *The Anointing of the Holy Spirit* (Ottawa, Canada: Bill Prankard Evangelistic Association).

How to Hear God's Voice

Books-

Jacobs, Cindy, *The Voice of God* (Ventura, Calif.: Regal Books from Gospel Light, 1995).

Pierce, Chuck D. and Pamela J., *One Thing* (Shippensburg, PA: Destiny Image Publishers Inc., 2006).

Pierce, Chuck D. and Wagner Sytsema, Rebecca, *When God Speaks* (Ventura, Calif.: Regal Books from Gospel Light, 2005).

Smith, Alice and Eddie, *Drawing Closer to God's Heart* (Lake Mary, Florida: Charisma House, Strang Communications Company, 2001).

CDs-

Chavda, Bonnie, *Hearing God* (Charlotte, NC, Morning Star Publications)

Jackson, John Paul, *The Art of Hearing from God* (North Sutton, NC: Streams Ministries International; a course offered either by correspondence or attendance) **

Johnson Bill, *Power of a Renewed Mind* (Redding, CA.: Bill Johnson Ministries) **

Identity-

Books-

Astin, Jill, *Dancing with Destiny* (Grand Rapids, MI: Chosen Books, 2007). **

Littauer, Florence, *Personality Plus* (Grand Rapids, MI: Fleming H. Revell, 1983). **

Kise, Jane A.G., Stark, David, and Hirsch Krebs, Sandra, *Discover Who You Are* (Minneapolis, Minnesota: Bethany House, 1996).

Myers, Isabel Briggs with Myers, Peter M. (Palo Alto, Calif.: 1980).

Wagner, C. Peter, *Your Spiritual Gifts* (Ventura, Calif: Regal Books, 1979). **

Justice

Books-

Colson, Charles, *Justice that Restores* (Wheaton, Illinois: Tyndale Publications, Inc., 2001).

Pierce, Chuck D. and Wagner Sytsema Rebecca, *The Future War of the Church* (Ventura, Calif.: Regal Books from Gospel Light, 2001).

Smith, Eddie and Alice, *The Advocates* (Lake Mary, Florida: Charisma House, Strang Communications Company, 2001). **

CDs-

Bentley, Todd, *Justice* (Abbotsford, B.C.: Fresh Fire Ministries)

Goll, James, *Judicial Intercession, Identifying and Capturing the Thief* (Tulsa, OK, Ministry to the Nations- DVD video)

Jackson, John Paul, *Keys to Receiving God's Justice* (N. Sutton, NH: Streams Ministries International) **

Jackson, John Paul, *Maximizing Heaven's Help* (N. Sutton, NH: Streams Ministries International) **

The Nations-

Books-

Petrie, Alistair, *Releasing Heaven on Earth* (Grand Rapids, MI.: Chosen Books, 2000).

Sandford, John Loren, *Healing the Nations—A Call to Global Intercession* (Grand Rapids, MI: Chosen Books, 2000). **

Silvoso, Ed, *That None Should Perish* (Ventura, Calif.: Regal Books, a division of Gospel Light, 1994).

Sheets, Dutch and Pierce, Chuck D., *Releasing the Prophetic Destiny of a Nation* (Shippensburg, PA.: Destiny Image Publishers Inc., 2005).

Prophecy-

Books-

Bickle, Mike, *Growing in the Prophetic* (Lake Mary, Florida: Charisma House, 1996).

Goll, James, *The Coming Prophetic Revolution* (Grand Rapids, MI: Chosen Books, 2001).

Goll, James, *The Seer* (Shippensburg, PA: Destiny Image Publishers Inc., 2004).

Hamon, Dr. Bill, Apostles, *Prophets and the Coming Move of God* (Shippensburg, PA.: Destiny Image Publishers, Inc., 1997).

Hamon, Dr. Bill, *Prophets and Personal Prophecy* (Shippensburg, PA.: Destiny Image Publishers, Inc., 1987).

Kingstone, Rodney, *Healing Earthbound Eagles* (Milton Keynes, England: Word Publishing, 2000).

Sandford, John and Paula, *The Elijah Task* (Tulsa, OK.: Victory House Inc., 1977).

Sandford, R. Loren, *Purifying the Prophetic* (Grand Rapids, MI: Chosen Books, 2005). **

Sandford, R. Loren, *Understanding Prophetic People* (Grand Rapids, MI: Chosen Books, 2007). **

Sparks, T. Austin, *Prophetic Ministry* (Shippensburg, PA: Destiny Image Publishing, Inc., 2000).

Thompson, Steve, *You May All Prophesy* (Fort Mill, SC: Morning Star Publications, 2000). **

CDs-

Jackson, John Paul, *Developing a Prophetic Community* (North Sutton, NH: Streams Ministries International- DVD)

Joyner, Rick, *The Prophetic Gifts* (Shippensburg, PA: Destiny Image)

Thompson, Steve, *Prophetic Training* (Charlotte, NC: Morning Star Publications

Spiritual Warfare

Books-

Annacondia, Carlos, *Listen to Me, Satan!* (Lake Mary, Florida: Creation House Strang Communications Company, 1998).

Frangipane, Francis, *The Three Battlegrounds* (Cedar Rapids, IA: Arrow Publications, 1989).

Frangipane, Francis, *This Day We Fight!* (Grand Rapids, MI: Chosen Books, 2005).

Jackson, John Paul, *Needless Casualties of War* (North Sutton, NH.: Streams Publishing House, 1999).**

Jacobs, Cindy, *Deliver Us From Evil* (Ventura, Calif.: Regal Books)

Joyner, Rick, *The Surpassing Greatness of His Great Power* (New Kensington, PA.: Whitaker House, 1996).

CDs-

Jackson, John Paul, *Effective Spiritual Warfare* (Dynamic Prayer Series, North Sutton, NH: Streams Ministries International) **

Joyner, Rick and other conference speakers, *Deliverance and Spiritual Warfare Conference*- APRIL 12-15/06 (Morning Star Ministries)

Watchmen

Books-

Lucia, Martha and Millar, Dana, *The Watchman* (Santa Rosa Beach, Florida: c/o Christian International Ministries Network, 2002).

CDS-

Hess, Tom, *Israel, Watch Men and the Church* (Charlotte, NC: Morning Star Publications)

** = HIGHLY RECOMMEND!!

End Notes

1. William Law, *A Serious Call to a Devout and Holy Life* (1728).
2. Paul Cain, *The Gift of Tears* (Kansas City, Mo.: Shiloh, 1997)
3. Jill Austin, *Awake, Deborah, Awake! Article from Master potter Ministries*
4. Eddie & Alice Smith, *Drawing Closer to God's Heart* (Lake Mary, FL.: Charisma House, 2001). 15
5. Andrew Murray, *Prayer: The Work of the Holy Spirit: God's Best Secrets* (Springdale, PA: Whitaker House, 1998), 56.
6. Chuck Pierce, *When God Speaks* (Ventura, Calif., Regal Books, 2005), 21
7. John & Paula Sandford, *God's Power to Change* (Lake Mary, Florida: Charisma House, 2007), 80.
8. R. Loren Sandford, *Understanding Prophetic People* (Grand Rapids, MI.: Chosen Books, 2007), 20-29.
9. Cindy Jacobs, *The Voice of God* (Ventura, Calif.: Regal Books, 1995), 39-40.
10. John Sandord, *Elijah Among Us* (Grand Rapids, MI: Chosen Books, 2002), 184
11. John & Paula Sandford, *The Elijah Task* (Tulsa, OK: Victory House, Inc. 1977), 132

12. James Goll, *Kneeling on the Promises* (Grand Rapids, MI.: Chosen Books, 1999),105-106.
13. T. Austin Sparks, *Prophetic Ministry* (Shippensburg, PA: Destiny Image, 2000), 2.
14. R. Loren Sandford, *Understanding Prophetic People* (Grand Rapids, MI.: Chosen Books, 2007), 85.

CAREER OPPORTUNITY

THE BODY OF CHRIST NEEDS YOU!!

The Body of Christ, the Church is desperately in need of committed intercessors who will position themselves, according to the will of the Lord, and will stand in the gap, to see the fulfillment of the Church's destiny. At present, there are thousands upon thousands of positions open. Many of these positions can lead to full time ministry in intercession and prophecy. These positions are what you have been created and destined for!

Required Skills:

Successful applicants will possess the following skills:
1. A hunger to see the Body of Christ fulfill the Great Commission.
2. A dependency upon the Lord in all things.
3. Willing to be schooled by the Holy Spirit.
4. A teachable, contrite spirit.
5. Willingness to give your time as needed and directed by the Holy Spirit.

Education/Experience:

All educational levels and experience will be considered!

Job locations:

All locations require intercessors, including all churches, businesses, cities and communities; some intercessors may need to re-locate as directed by the Holy Spirit.

Benefits:

1. Lifelong learning and advancement.
2. Many intercessors will go on to a prophetic ministry.
3. A life of abundance!

> "And the grace of our Lord was exceedingly abundant, with faith and love which are in Christ Jesus" (1Timothy 1:14 NKJ).

4. Heavenly rewards!

> "We give thanks to the God and Father of our Lord Jesus Christ, praying always for you, since we heard of your faith in Christ Jesus and of your love for all the saints; because of the hope which is laid up for you in heaven" (Colossians 1:3-5 NKJ).

5. Living from glory to glory!

> "And that He might make known the riches of His glory on the vessels of mercy" (Romans 9:23 NKJ).

6. Joy!

> "But rejoice to the extent that you partake of Christ's sufferings, that when His glory is revealed, you may also be glad with exceeding joy" (1 Peter 4:13 NKJ).

How to apply:

Pray:

Dear Lord, I desire to become an intercessor, or to become a more, committed intercessor. I confess right now, that I am desperate for You. I want to know your sufferings and grow in wisdom in all things, especially in intercession, God. Help me. I need to discern between soul and spirit. I need healing so that I no longer have a wounded, hardened heart. I repent before You, God, that I have taken on burdens that You did not want me to carry. Forgive me for allowing Satan to speak lies regarding intercession and who I am and for being critical in my responses to Your children or not responding at all. I declare right now, that my identity is in You, and You have called me to stand in the gap, and to be moved by compassion, as You are, Jesus. Dwell in me, Holy Spirit.

Impart and stir up a gift of intercession. Teach me, Holy Spirit in prayer and intercession. I ask that You position me geographically and relationally exactly where You want me, God. In Jesus' name. Amen.

_____, (Your Name)
Intercessor, History maker!

My prayer for you:

To those who desire to walk in the fullness of their calling and identity as an intercessor: Lord, I pray that You use these people mightily. Protect them from Satan; shield them, God. Keep them focused on You, Lord. Remove distractions from their lives. Lord, I ask for quick response to their prayers to encourage them. I ask for spiritual mothers and fathers to mature those beginning this walk of intercession. I ask that for those who are called to be spiritual mothers or fathers You would bring children to them to mentor and teach. Bless them, their families and loved ones, Lord. In Jesus' name. Amen.

Please send any prayer requests to: careys@sasktel.net

LaVergne, TN USA
12 February 2010
172963LV00001B/77/P